W9-ASX-182

KIDS GARDEN!

The Anytime, Anyplace Guide to Sowing & Growing Fun

Avery Hart and Paul Mantell

Illustrations by Loretta Braren and Jennie Chien

"Offers a bountiful harvest of gardening activities indoors and out, as well as practical tips and advice."
— *Publishers Weekly*

WILLIAMSON PUBLISHING CO. CHARLOTTE, VERMONT

Kids Can! and *Little Hands* are registered trademarks of Williamson Publishing Company.

Library of Congress
Cataloging-in-Publication Data
Hart, Avery
  Kids garden!: the anytime, anyplace guide to
    sowing & growing fun
  /Avery Hart & Paul Mantell.
        p.   cm.
    ISBN 0-913589-90-X
    1. Gardening—Juvenile literature. 2. Indoor
gardening—Juvenile literature. [1. Gardening.
2. Indoor gardening.]   I. Mantell, Paul II. Title.
    SB457.H35 1995
    635—dc20   94-44851
                                                          CIP
Kids Can! ® Series editor: Susan Williamson   AC

Cover and interior design: Trezzo-Braren Studio
Illustrations: Loretta Braren and Jennie Chien
Printing: Capital City Press

Williamson Publishing Co.
P.O. Box 185
Charlotte, Vermont 05445
(800) 234-8791

Manufactured in the United States of America
24 23 22 21 20 19 18 17 16 15 14 13 12 11

A Williamson *Kids Can!* Book

If you want to be happy your whole life long, be a gardener.

OLD CHINESE SAYING

DEDICATION

This book is dedicated to everybody who loves the earth and takes care of it.

CONTENTS

ACKNOWLEDGEMENTS

Grateful thanks to Irene Brino Wagner, Susan Williamson, Geoff and Sarah Harden, Clayton and Matthew Mantell, Mary Schulherr, Ardica Williams, and the man who lives next to the pizza place on Route 209.

ABOUT THE AUTHORS

Avery Hart and Paul Mantell are the authors of numerous other books including Williamson Publishing's *Kids & Weekends: Creative Ways to Make Special Days* and *Kids Make Music!: Clapping and Tapping from Bach to Rock!*

A PERFECT PARTNERSHIP

PLANTING YOURSELF IN A GARDEN

Instead of words, we wanted a fragrant hyacinth to pop up, right under your nose, the minute you opened this book! We wanted a cherry tomato to jump off the page and into your mouth, bringing all its zesty, tangy taste to you.

We wanted to hand you a clump of clean, woodsy dirt to feel and smell. And we hoped we could fill your home with fresh garden air every time you leaf through these pages.

Instead we did the best we could with words. So, you'll find the hyacinths on page 91, and tomatoes on page 71. You'll come across dirt on page 38. But the real magic, the kind of magic we've just described, will come from your plants.

That's because Mother Nature and Father Time have secrets that they share only with gardeners. As you garden, those secrets come silently to you, adding to your wisdom and power. You realize, in a brand-new yet ancient way, that the whole earth is a garden, waiting for our love and care. Knowing that changes you forever.

So get ready to get growing, and discover a miracle that's close to your bones. Plants and flowers aren't the only ones who get to bloom in a garden, you know.

People do, too!

PLANTS AND PEOPLE

When you team up with a plant, you make a perfect partnership. For one thing plants breathe out the oxygen that people breathe in; people breathe out the carbon dioxide that plants breathe in. And like any good friendship, plants make our world a nicer place to live in. People take good care of their plants by watering them and placing them in a sunny (or shady if that's what the plant likes) spot. Give and take — plus lots of love and under-standing — that's what makes the perfect plant and people partnership!

INNIE OR OUTIE?

Are you an Innie or an Outie? No, we're not asking about your belly button! We're asking where your garden grows — indoors or out? Chances are, you're both!

You may be an Innie this year because you live in the city, and an Outie next year when you move to the country or suburbs. Or you may be an Outie in the summer and an Innie in the winter.

Check the Index for a list of Innie garden activities. And if you want to be an Outie but have no place to garden where you live, write to the *American Community Gardening Association*, 325 Walnut St., Philadelphia, PA 19106 (215-546-8455). They can put you in touch with your home city's community gardening organization. There's an outdoor garden in your future!

MAKE A PLANT PERSON

You can make a comical "plant person" with a full head of gorgeous, green "hair." Your plant person can sit on a saucer in your kitchen. As you munch your breakfast, watch its head go from bald to bushy!

YOU'LL NEED:

Old nylon stocking

Sawdust (or vermiculite, perlite, or soil)

2 tablespoons (25 ml) of grass seed

Thumbtacks and twist tie

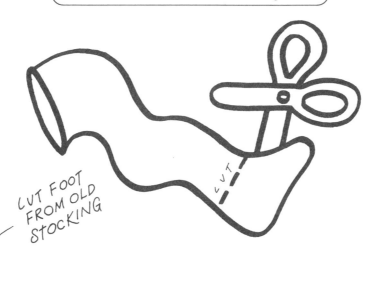

CUT FOOT FROM OLD STOCKING

PLACE 2 TABLESPOONS OF GRASS SEED IN TOE

FILL FOOT WITH SAWDUST; THEN SECURE WITH TWIST TIE

MOISTEN EVERY DAY AND KEEP IN A SUNNY SPOT

Cut the foot from an old nylon stocking and pour the grass seed into the toe. Add sawdust until the foot is full. Tie the stocking tightly at the opening with a twist tie, place on a saucer twist-tie end down, and shape into a round head.

Push in thumbtacks for eyes, nose, and mouth, or cut these from cloth and attach with straight pins.

Soak your plant person with water and place it in a sunny spot. Moisten it every day. When the "hair" grows, give your plant person a hairdo like a flattop or a shag cut.

GOOD MORNING, DIANTHUS!

Plants have names, and just like people, they often have both a formal name and a nickname, or common name.

Take Sweet William. That's the common name of the fragrant garden flower who's formally known as *Dianthus barbatus*.

Plants get their nicknames because someone noticed something special about them long ago. For instance, an English speaker must have once seen *Bellis perennis* and said, "That flower is as bright as the day's eye!" "Day's Eye," meaning sun, was repeated so often, it turned into "daisy!"

The "poppy" flower got its name because of the "popping" sound people make when chewing poppy seeds. Can you imagine how plants such as the zebra plant, butter-and-eggs, prayer plant, lamb's ears, elephant-ear fern, and foxglove might have gotten their names?

Science Sense

Plants are not the only creatures with scientific, Latin names. There's also *Tyrannosaurus rex* and *Stegosaurus*. And if you walk to a mirror and grin, you'll even see a *Homo sapiens* smiling back at you!

DO PLANTS HAVE FEELINGS?

For ages, people have tried to answer this question. After all, plants are alive and growing, and they definitely respond to attention and love.

Imagine being a plant: Try being a plant in your imagination. Take off your shoes, close your eyes, and "plant" your feet firmly on the ground.

Let your toes "grab" the ground, and imagine they are sending roots deep into the soil in search of food and water. Feel that fuel moving up into your body.

Is the sun shining on you? Let your arms reach up, and feel its life-giving warmth. Do you hear birds in the trees? What else do you hear?

Here comes a big wind! It's a good thing you are rooted to the ground! Bend and sway, plant!

WIZARD OF THE WOODS

One person who understood plants was George Washington Carver, the world-famous botanist who lived about a hundred years ago.

As a kid, Carver went to a secret spot in the woods where he'd listen to the sounds of nature. He once said, "I learn what I know by watching and loving everything. Flowers talk to me, and so do little living things in the woods. Anyone who loves enough, and believes, can know these secrets."

Listen to a plant: Can you sense any silent messages coming from the trees and plants near you? To find out, do what Carver did — listen!

Sit or stand in front of a plant you like, and take a quiet moment to open yourself up to its life. Then silently ask if the plant has any message for you. You may be surprised by the results! Then, read Shel Silverstein's *The Giving Tree*. Does it change how you think about plants and people?

READY, SET, GROW!

Here's some gardening you can do right now. There's a garden in your kitchen that's waiting for you to bring it to life!

COOK UP A KITCHEN-SCRAP GARDEN

To see nature in action, head for your kitchen. You can raise a beanstalk there, or a tree, or a potful of carrot tops to give to a red-headed friend. All you need are fruit and vegetable scraps, potting soil (see page 38), and containers (see page 102).

P.S.!

Plant a few of each of these kitchen projects. That way, if one is a dud (and some will be!), you'll still have others to enjoy.

GROW A BEANSTALK

The dried beans in your pantry, like navy, kidney, lima, or lentil beans, are actually seeds you can plant. A kidney or pole bean will zoom up like Jack's famous beanstalk when you give it a tall stick to climb on. You can cut out a paper-person to put among the leaves of the plant. That's Jack. As for the giant, it's you! (For more bean seed ideas, see pages 64–67.)

AVOCADO-PIT TREE

The first step to growing a lush, leafy avocado tree is eating avocados — those golden-green vegetables for salads, sandwiches, or eaten as a dip called guacamole.

Wash the very big pit (seed), and then stick three toothpicks around its middle. Place in a glass of water with the narrow top up, and the fat bottom under the water. (Add water as needed to keep the bottom wet.)

In a week or so, you'll see slender roots reach down into the water, as stems shoot up from the top of the pit! Congratulations! Your baby avocado tree has sprouted! When it has two sets of leaves, plant it in soil. Place in the sunniest spot in the house. In warm climates, plant the tree outside; by the time you're twenty, it will be much bigger than you!

Guacamole

Dip corn chips, carrot sticks, and cucumber slices into a bowl of guacamole (GWA-ca-MOH-lay), a Mexican avocado dish. It's great for fiestas or any old time!

YOU'LL NEED:

2 ripe avocados (avocados are ripe when they are soft to the touch and their skins are blackish)

1 teaspoon (5 ml) lemon or lime juice

1 tablespoon (25 ml) mayonnaise

1 tablespoon (25 ml) salsa (To grow a salsa garden, see page 57.)

Mash the ingredients together and enjoy!

BRIGHT GREEN THUMB

Give It a Shape

Your avocado plant can grow as a tree or a bush. To make a tree, let the plant grow freely. To make a bush, snip off the top of the plant when the "trunk" gets about a foot high (1/3 meter). The plant will then branch out.

HOMEGROWN LEMON AND ORANGE TREES

Okay, we admit it: You can't drink orange juice from these home-grown oranges. And forget sipping lemonade made from your lemons. That's because the fruits of these houseplants are only the size of marbles.

But if you like white flowers and dark shiny leaves, and if the clean, fresh scent of orange or lemon gives you a good feeling, you'll love growing a citrus plant!

Start by eating an orange or using some lemons. Save the seeds (pits). Let them dry for a day or two before you plant them in moist, rich soil. Put a few Popsicle sticks around the edge of the pot and cover with clear plastic. Your baby citrus plant needs lots of light and warmth.

Keep the soil moist, and in time you'll see a stem poking through the soil. When you see leaves, remove the plastic and watch your new tree grow, grow, grow!

PLASTIC WRAP

CARROT TOPS

Carrot tops are lacy, graceful plants that you can grow in the kitchen. Start by buying — or growing! — carrots *with the greens still attached.* Cut off the leaves, leaving just a little green. Munch the carrots, leaving a small piece of orange.

Plant the carrot tops in a soil-filled container, keep them moist, and wait. In a week or two you will see a fringe of new curly green growth sprouting from the top. If you have a stuffed rabbit, set it next to the pot!

PRETTY USEFUL

Beet tops and turnip tops make leafy green plants, too. Grow them the same way you grow carrot tops.

SWEET POTATO VINE

You can have a string of leaves climbing around your kitchen with a sweet potato vine. Put a sweet potato in a glass of water, half in and half out, and add water from time to time. Soon a vine will begin growing — and what a vine! If you are super-lucky, the vine may produce the beautiful, lilac-colored sweet potato flower.

POPCORN PIE

Popcorn kernels are seeds, too. Fill a pie plate with potting soil and plant the kernels. Keep the soil moist and soon you'll have a light green popcorn pie!

PINEAPPLE CROWN

You can't wear this crown, but a saucer can. Just slice off the crown (top) of a pineapple, and set it in a dish of water. New leaves and roots will form. Plant the crown in a container of sandy soil, and it will look nice for a long time. Plant in soil and it may grow a golfball-sized pineapple someday!

THE AMAZING DISAPPEARING LETTUCE LEAF

Imagine taking a large lettuce leaf and making it disappear without a trace! How will you perform this amazing feat?

By using Mother Nature's Break-Down Magic! Take a leaf outside, tear it up in pieces, and put them on the ground (or in a pot of soil). Cover them with dirt, sprinkle with water, and wait.

A week or two later, go dig up that leaf. Alacazamm! It won't be there! It disappeared into the soil, as *compost*! (See page 38.)

GARDEN MAGIC

Welcome to Mother Nature's Magic Show — starring YOU! Gardening just may be the greatest magic of all time. And once you start growing, you, too, will discover the secrets behind the magic.

THE FANTASTIC HOUSE-PLANT PERK-UP ACT

To perform this magic act, you'll need a droopy houseplant and a glass of water. With great flourish in the best magician's tradition, pour the water into the soil, and wait a few hours. Whammo-Kazammo! The plant will perk up, refreshed and alert! (For more amazing houseplants, see page 95.)

THE STUPENDOUS TRANSFORMING TULIP TRICK

As a gardening magician, you can take a plain, lumpy bulb and transform it into an awesome, blooming beauty!

Simply set a tulip bulb in a pot of soil, cover with more soil, and with much waving of hands and flashing of a colorful handkerchief, say the magic word, *"Patience!"*

Keep the soil watered, and, in time, that plain bulb will become a magnificent blooming flower! (See page 87.) Wow! What magic powers you have, garden!

We're Proud to Present . . .
LIGHT, WATER, AND TEMPERATURE

Like all magicians, you'll need assistants, of course. As a gardener, you get three — light, water, and temperature. Learning to use them and work with them will turn your thumb a bright, magical green!

HERE COMES THE SUN!

Do you tend to feel cheerful on a sunny day? Plants seem to perk up in the sun, too. In fact, plants absolutely need sunlight to grow and thrive. But finding the best light for your plants will take some detective work!

No matter where you stand, the sun always travels in a path from east (in the morning) to west (in the afternoon).

Wherever light comes from — east, south, or west — is called exposure. Southern exposures are best for most plants, because the sun takes hours to cross the southern sky in the northern hemisphere.

Make a sun map: Take a sheet of white paper and pretend it is your garden, or the room your plants will be in. Draw your garden, house, or furniture. Then get some yellow, orange, and red crayons ready.

In the morning, look around your growing space. Ask yourself, "Where is the sun shining?" Go to the paper and fill in yellow stripes where you see the sun shining.

Do the same in the early afternoon (about 1 PM) with orange stripes, and late afternoon (about 4 or 5 PM) with red stripes. If the sun shines in the same place more than once in a day, put more stripes there, too.

Now you have a map of where the sun shines in your growing space - indoors or out! The place with the brightest yellow-red-orange plaid will be the sunniest place for plants.

BRIGHT GREEN THUMB

All Shade?

If your house or yard is shady all day, don't worry! Just grow shade-loving plants (see page 128). You can even create a special shady farm!

PLANTING BY THE MOON

Does moonlight affect plants? Some people think so. They plant their gardens according to the position of the moon! Other people think the whole idea is, well, loony. (The Latin word for moon is *luna*, by the way — that's where the term loony came from.)

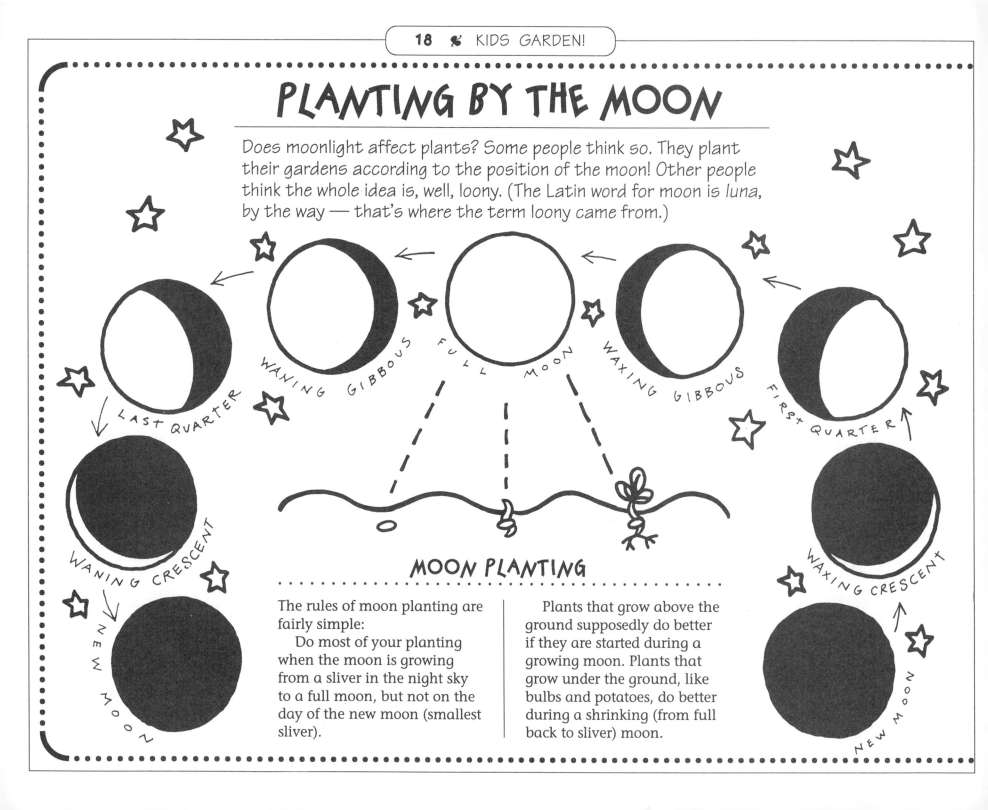

LAST QUARTER

WANING GIBBOUS

FULL MOON

WAXING GIBBOUS

FIRST QUARTER

WANING CRESCENT

NEW MOON

WAXING CRESCENT

NEW MOON

MOON PLANTING

The rules of moon planting are fairly simple:

Do most of your planting when the moon is growing from a sliver in the night sky to a full moon, but not on the day of the new moon (smallest sliver).

Plants that grow above the ground supposedly do better if they are started during a growing moon. Plants that grow under the ground, like bulbs and potatoes, do better during a shrinking (from full back to sliver) moon.

USEFUL OR "LUN"-Y?

You can decide for yourself if moon planting works, by experimenting with dry bean seeds, like kidney, lima, or navy beans.

YOU'LL NEED:

10 bean seeds and a place to plant them

Notepaper and pencil

Plant five seeds when the moon is growing, and five seeds when the moon is shrinking. For each group of seeds, write down the dates you planted, when they sprouted, and how fast they grew. Water them equally well.

Did the new-moon seeds sprout in fewer days? Did one group appear healthier? Do you think planting by the moon works?

WANING MOON

WAXING MOON

WHEN DOES YOUR GARDEN GROW?

Different places have different growing seasons. If you live in Florida, you can plant vegetables outside in March. But if you live in Canada, you'll have to wait until May!

That's because northern gardeners have to wait for the frost date to pass. The frost date tells gardeners when their gardens will be safe from any freezing. Visit the library or a garden nursery and look up the frost dates for where you live. You'll see that zone 1 is the coldest (and having the shortest growing season) on up to zone 11 with the longest growing season.

BRIGHT GREEN THUMB

Perfect Timing

People who garden a lot have clever ways to find when their gardens are safe from frost. Try some of these:

One old-time gardener says to lie down without a coat where you will plant. If it's uncomfortable for you, don't plant yet!

Here's a tip from an 80-year-old gardener: Wait till the weeds start to grow, then plant.

Or you can give your soil the "footprint test": Step on the soil and then examine the footprint. If it's shiny, it's too early to plant!

A LIVING CIRCLE

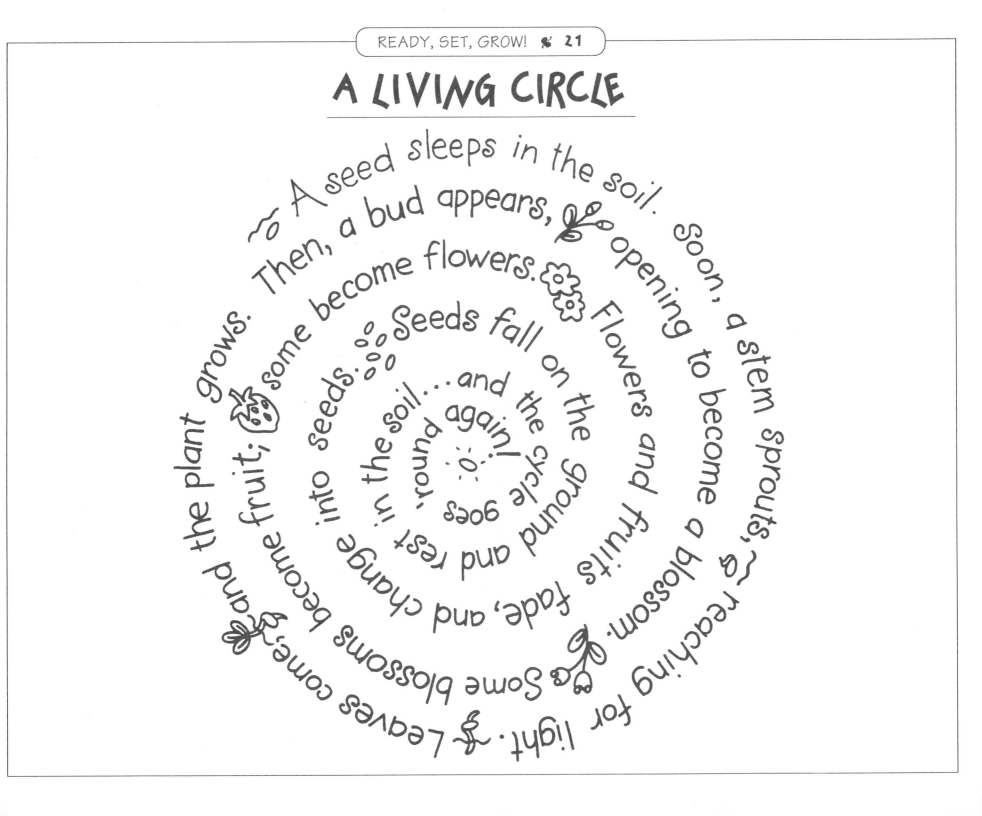

A seed sleeps in the soil. Soon, a stem sprouts, reaching for light. Leaves come, and the plant grows. Then, a bud appears, opening to become a blossom. Some blossoms become flowers. Some become fruits. Flowers and fruits fade, and change into seeds. Seeds fall on the ground and rest in the soil...and the cycle goes 'round, 'round again!

WATER — JUST THE RIGHT AMOUNT

Water! Without it, plants die; with too much of it, they drown. With just enough, they grow and flourish! One of your most important jobs as a gardener is making sure your plants get the water they need — the way they need it!

Science Sense

Seeing Is Believing

To see how important the right amount of water is, try this experiment:

1 Take nine bean seeds, and put three of them on three different saucers.

2 Keep the seeds on the first saucer soaked thoroughly.

3 Place the seeds in the second saucer, on a moist paper towel. Sprinkle them with water every day, keeping them moist.

4 In the third saucer, leave the seeds dry.

5 Place all saucers in a dark place and wait about a week. Make sure the first saucer stays soaked, the second moist, and the third dry.

The results will tell you a lot about how the right amount of water affects seeds.

SAUCER #1
SOAK BEANS AND KEEP WET

YOU'LL NEED:

9 dried beans

3 saucers

Paper towel or cotton cloth

SAUCER #2
KEEP BEANS ON MOIST PAPER TOWEL

SAUCER #3
KEEP BEANS DRY

MAKE A RAIN STICK

Native people of the Amazon jungle use rain sticks — hollow tubes that imitate the sound of falling rain — in an effort to coax the water out of the sky. To make your rain stick, find the longest, thickest tube in the house. Paper towel tubes are okay, but tennis ball holders or poster mailers are better — and bamboo stalks are best of all!

← GROCERY BAG BOTTOM

← CARDBOARD TUBE

← RUBBER BAND

YOU'LL NEED:

Long, cardboard tube

Paint or gift wrap

Brown grocery bag

Rubber bands

Box of toothpicks, some rice, and tissues

1 Decorate the outside of the rain stick by painting it, or covering it with art paper or gift wrap. Some artists paint clouds, rain, and plants with acrylics or watercolors. Some make zigzags or other kinds of designs.

2 While the tube is drying, make tube ends by cutting circles at least 3 inches (10 cm) larger than the tube from the double-thick bottom of a grocery bag.

3 To make the sound of rain, add a big bunch of toothpicks, some crushed tissues, and some dry rice to the tube. Attach the ends with strong rubber bands, and turn the tube over slowly. Listen to the soothing sound of falling rain!

A GREENER WORLD
Pure and Simple

Plants need poison-free water just as much as people do. To see how plants soak up water, take a stick of celery and cut off the bottom with a sharp knife (have a grown-up help you). Place the celery in a glass of water, add some food coloring, and wait. What happened? Now imagine that the color was really the poison of pollution. See how it spreads throughout the plant. Clean water and air are important to all life — plants included! (See "Be a Botanist," page 24.)

A LIVING LABORATORY

If you love science, a garden is a great place to be. Think of it as a living laboratory, teeming with challenges and mysteries about how and why plants behave the way they do.

BE A BOTANIST!

A *botanist* (BAH-ta-nist) is a scientist who studies plant life. With a bunch of bean seeds, you can be a botanist and expand your knowledge of what makes plants grow.

Three curiosity ticklers:

1 Take three bean seeds and "plant" them on a plate in the refrigerator. Give them the moisture they need to germinate, and then observe what happens.

2 Do plants really grow better if you talk to them? Experiment by planting two seeds and giving them the same good conditions for growing (water, light, temperature). Talk to one seed, and ignore the other one. Any difference in the results?

3 How bad is pollution for plants? Take two bean seedlings in different containers to find out. When you water them, water one with clean water, and the other with diet soda and blue window cleaner. Watch for results.

PLANT MAZE

Did you ever notice that plants stretch in the direction of the light? This is called *phototropism* (foh-toh-TROHP-iz-im). To discover just how determined plants are to find light, make this plant maze.

YOU'LL NEED:

Small carton or large shoe box

Small flowerpot filled with potting soil

1 or 2 runner-bean seeds

Cardboard

1 Cut a hole in one end of the box. Add two pieces of cardboard inside with holes in them, too, creating a maze for the bean seedling.

2 Plant the seed about an inch (2.4 cm) deep in the pot, and keep it moist so it can sprout.

3 Place the pot on the other side of the box from the hole to give that little seed a challenge! Keep the box covered, with light entering only through the end hole.

Did your plants reach for the sun? How do you think they knew where to go?

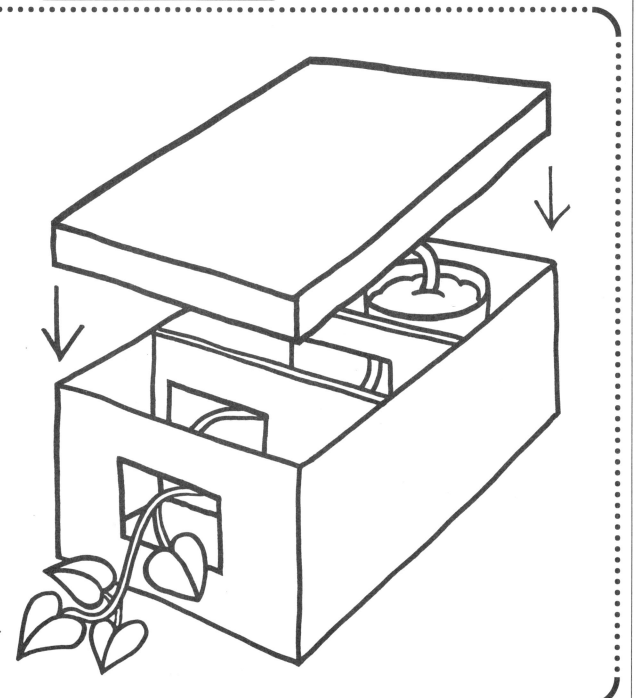

PLANNING AND PLOTTING

Planning and plotting a garden is part dream work and part math! The dream part is imagining what you want to grow, and how cool your garden will be. The math part is figuring out how much room you have to make your dream come true!

A garden can be whatever you choose: from a strawberry patch to a flowery window box to a miniature farm on your deck. Some seed companies offer kids special "one-cent" rates! What a bargain!

But remember, like you, your garden will be unique — no two gardens are ever totally alike. And, however well you plan it, count on nature throwing you a few surprises! The basil may flop, or the impatiens may go wild!

HERBS

RADISH
SEEDS

FLOWER
SEEDS

BRIGHT GREEN THUMB

Mixing and matching food and flower gardens is more than fun — it can be practical, too. Marigolds at the edge of a vegetable garden will help keep pests away! (See "Trouble in Paradise," page 143.)

TALL PLANTS IN BACK

SHORT PLANTS IN FRONT

PLOTTING

When wintertime is wondrous white,
Plan your summertime garden right.

Plotting a garden means planning on paper. When you plot you make a map, or design, of what you want to grow, showing how you will arrange the plants. Innies can plan and plot an indoor growing-space according to how much shelf space, how much sunlight, and how many containers they have.

YOU'LL NEED:

Tape measure

Ruler

Paper (graph paper is best)

Measure your garden area and draw its outline to *scale*. For instance, one inch on paper can stand for one foot in the garden.

Use your math to help you plot by multiplying the length by the width of the garden. If your garden is 6 feet by 6 feet (2 m x 2 m), for instance, you will have 36 square feet (4 sq. m) to plant.

The basic rule is one plant for every square foot. Your 36-square-foot garden, for example, will be able to support about 36 plants — fewer if you choose big plants, like corn, and more if you choose small plants, like pansies.

When you plot, put low-growing plants in front and taller ones in the back. Gardeners have to get into their gardens to weed and water, too. Leave room for yourself! (Look for sample plots on pages 56 – 57.)

COMPANION GARDENING

Certain plants seem to enjoy growing together, but others don't get along. Choosing the right plants to grow together is called *companion planting.*

Plants send out natural chemical signals that are harmonious and friendly — to their pals, that is. So when deciding what to plant where, keep these likes and dislikes in mind.

FRIENDS:

Corn, Peas, and Cucumbers

Parsley and Tomatoes

Spinach and Strawberries

Carrots and Beans

Marigolds and Tomatoes

NOT-SO-FRIENDLY:

Pumpkins and Potatoes

Cucumbers and Potatoes

Basil and Rue

TOOLS OF THE TRADE

Having good tools really makes a difference in gardening. Here's a list of what you'll need to get growing. Be sure to include a *magnifying glass* in your tool kit, too. That way, the tiniest wonders of nature will be plain to see!

A *rake* smooths the ground and makes it level.

A *hoe* is good for chopping up lumps in the soil.

tools for Outies
(OUTDOOR GARDENERS)

A *spade* is good for digging.

A *trowel* is a hand-held spade.

A *watering can* or *hose* brings water to the garden.

A *wheelbarrow* is good for trips to the compost and carrying garden supplies — but best for rides!

A *hat* with a wide brim protects your face from too much sun, and *gloves* protect your hands.

tools for innies
(INDOOR GARDENERS)
. . . .

Fingers or old forks can serve as rakes.

Old serving spoons make good trowels.

A *watering can* — the kind with a long, slender spout — helps you help your plants.

Empty, clean spray bottles are good for misting. Most plants enjoy a shower every now and then!

Plant stands lift your house-plants to show them off. (One easy plant stand is another flowerpot, turned upside down.)

Containers and pots make excellent planters as long as they hold water.

Coasters or pieces of cork or tiles protect shelves from water stains.

A GREENER WORLD

A Sneaker Planter!

Old shoes and sneakers make fun plant containers for Innies. Pack the shoe with soil, plant, place in a sunny location, and water at the ankle. Your plant will be too happy in its shoe house to ever run away.

DIG A HOLE, PLANT A SEED

Be patient, O be patient!
Put your ear against the earth;
Listen there how noiselessly
The germ of the seed has birth.

WILLIAM LINTON

GROW, LITTLE SEED!

Seeds are amazing! In every
one lies the complete plan for
a living plant, plus all the food
that plant needs to get started!
Seeds only need the right
conditions — warmth, dark,
and moisture — to sprout out
of their shells.

Most sprouts live on the
food and energy inside the
seed until they get their second
set of leaves and become
seedlings. That's when they
need to be planted in soil.
(See transplanting, page 36.)

FIRST FOLIAGE

GROWING PLANT

LEAF STALK

EPICOTYL

SEED COAT

FOOD

PRIMARY ROOT

LATERAL ROOT

SOIL

BRIGHT GREEN THUMB

Plant seeds about
three times as deep
as they are fat. Tiny
seeds need only a
little soil scattered
over them.

A JUMP-START GARDEN

You can jump-start your outdoor garden by planting seeds inside in late winter. Plant in peat pots, which are special containers made from peat moss, or any other planter (see page 102). An empty egg carton is a good seedling tray for tiny seeds, too. Starting seeds indoors means you'll have more time to enjoy your garden.

YOU'LL NEED:

Seeds

Containers to plant in

Potting soil

PEAT POT

EGG CARTON

YOGURT CUP

MILK CARTON

Plant the seeds and place the containers in the sunniest spot in your house. (You may want to use some grow lights on your seeds. Ask at a hardware store.) Keep the seeds moist. Once the baby plants sprout and grow two sets of leaves, they are officially *seedlings*. When the weather gets sunny and warmer, set your seedlings outside for an hour or two, so they gradually get used to being outside. That's called *hardening off*.

When the weather is warm enough (see seed packet instructions for exact temperatures), your seedlings will be ready for planting!

Science Sense

Weight-Lifting Seeds

To get an idea of how powerful a little seed can be, try planting a bean seed and then covering it with a coin. Keep the soil moist. When the seed sprouts, it will lift up the coin, and push it over!

SPROUTING ONE, TWO, THREE!

Sprouts are a crunchy power food that are incredibly easy to grow. All you need are dry seeds, water, a bowl, and a dark place for the seeds to germinate and sprout. You can sprout any of these: alfalfa, mung, soy, lima, pinto, garbanzo, barley, mustard, sesame, or oat seeds.

1 Put several dozen seeds in a bowl and barely cover them with water.

2 Cover the bowl, put it in the dark, and wait a few days.

3 Rinse and eat! (If you sprouted big seeds, snip off the sprouts with scissors.)

Bean Sprout and Avocado Hero

Use two pieces of crusty Italian bread, a thick slice of ripe avocado, a handful of sprouts, a slice of tomato, and a thin smear of mayonnaise or tahini sauce to make the yummiest sandwich ever.

A SEEDLING GREENHOUSE

Greenhouses, places where plants can get extra sun, warmth, and moisture, are made of glass or see-through plastic. Making a mini-greenhouse for your young plants will get them off to a great start!

YOU'LL NEED:

Carton

Dry-cleaning bag, or plastic wrap

Ask a grown-up to help you cut off the top flaps of the carton, and cut large windows in every side. Cover the top and side openings with clear plastic taped to the box.

Your greenhouse will let in sunlight and keep out chilly winds. Perfect for young seedlings!

LET'S GET PLANTING

DIGGING THE HOLE

A good bit of gardening wisdom says to dig a ten-dollar hole for every ten-cent plant! The hole you dig has to last the plant's entire life, so dig deep and wide! Add compost or manure to the bottom of the hole before you plant, too. (See "Compost," page 39.) That's like packing lunch for your plant to eat when it gets hungry and you aren't there!

Super gardeners water the hole before and after they plant. Even little plants need lots of water when they're in a new home. Set the plant in the hole, and fill in soil all around it. Pat down the soil with your hand to remove any air holes.

THIN THEM OUT

When too many seeds sprout, thin them out by pulling or cutting some of the sprouts. Plants need room. If you try to let them all live, they'll all die!

If you are thinning lettuce or carrot seedlings, don't let them go to waste, though. Rinse them and pop them in your mouth for a quick snack!

P.S.!

The secret of transplanting (putting a seedling into the earth) is: Handle the seedling by the leaves, *not the stem*. If a leaf breaks, the plant will grow a new one. But if the stem breaks, it's goodbye, Charley!

PICK UP SEEDLING BY THE LEAVES

DIG HOLE DEEP AND WIDE

CELEBRATE!

With Good Wishes

Native people everywhere take a moment to wish their plants well when they set them in the ground. We tried it in our garden and it works!

As you plant, tell the seed or seedling that you want it to grow healthy and strong. Plants have a mysterious way of responding to people's hopes for them.

BE A SEED SAVER

Saving seeds is a quiet but powerful way to help Mother Nature. Here's why: Over the years, people have begun to farm fewer and fewer kinds of foods. Ninety percent of what most people eat comes from just twenty species. And out of those twenty, corn, rice, and potatoes account for over half of all food eaten!

Giant agricultural businesses grow millions of acres of these dependable crops. They need to grow foods that will all ripen at the same time, and that will travel well. Good enough, but it leaves something out of the story.

That missing something is *diversity*, or having many different kinds of plants and foods. Lack of diversity is not only boring, it could mean big trouble. Because if a disease ever hits the common food plants all at once, people could starve!

Lack of diversity also means that some very special plants get lost along the road to "progress." Grandma's roses that smell superbly sweet and Uncle Ralph's prize purple pole beans could become ancient history!

Is there a special plant that you think should continue? If so, save its seeds!

ZEBRA-STRIPED TOMATOES?

You and your family or school can join other seed savers. The Seed Savers Exchange (3076 North Winn Road, Decorah, Iowa 52101) is a nonprofit group dedicated to keeping lots of different plants growing. If you are in Iowa, you can visit their Heritage Farm from June to September.

If you live in the Southwest, you can order seeds of plants traditionally grown by the Southwest native people, like Hopi rattle gourds, or giant white sunflowers from Native Seeds/Search at 2509 North Campbell Avenue #325, Tucson, Arizona 85719.

If you live in the mid-Atlantic United States, send for a free catalog of old-fashioned and unusual plants, such as chocolate popcorn and green zebra-striped tomatoes! (Southern Exposure, P.O. Box 170, Earysville, Virginia 22936.)

THE GOOD EARTH

THE SOIL SPEAKS: "I'M ALIVE!"

"Go ahead and step on me. I'm used to it. But it doesn't change the fact that I'm alive! That's right — I'm as alive as you are!

"Not only that, I've got a big job! I deliver the right mix of elements that plants need to make food. I make sure plant roots get air and water, too. I guess you could call me part chemist and part mother.

"So go ahead, put your hands in me and give me a tickle now and then. Put your nose down and give me a little sniff. Later, you can wash me off your hands. Until then, while you're in the garden, or inside, potting plants, please, let's stay in touch!"

MEET SOME MICROBES

Microbes (MY-krohbs) are tiny creatures such as protozoa, fungi, and bacteria that can be seen only with a microscope. They keep soil healthy.

In a spoonful of healthy soil there are about a hundred thousand protozoa, thirty million fungi, and two billion bacteria! Just because they're small doesn't mean they are unimportant, though. Without microbes, nothing would grow!

Look at a microbe swimming pool: When it comes to microbes, seeing is believing. And you can see them for yourself if you look under a microscope.

Fill a small jar with pond water. In just one drop, you'll see little one-celled creatures wiggling and swimming. Those are the water-loving cousins of the microbes in the soil!

After you look in the microscope, try drawing the creatures you saw.

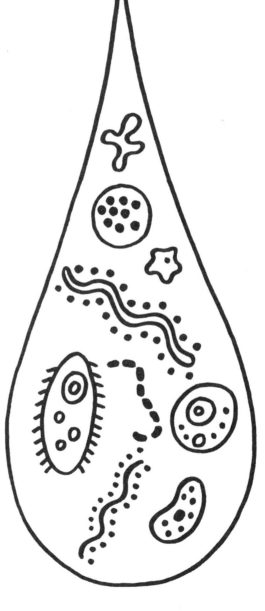

BRIGHT GREEN THUMB

Perfect Potting Soil

For perfect potting soil, mix one part soil, one part compost, and one part vermiculite. Vermiculite is air-popped mica, a very light rock. Because it's been "popped" under heat, the air space inside the grains allows room for air, food, and water in the soil.

Vermiculite is as light as a feather — something you will appreciate when you lift your potted plants!

MUD-PIE TIME!

To grow a great garden, it's wise to know what kind of soil you have. And the best way to discover that information is by making good old mud pies by adding a little water to a handful of dirt.

★ If your mud pie is heavy and sticky, and forms a solid clump, your soil has clay in it.

★ If your mud pie falls apart, and just won't keep its shape after you pat it, your soil is sandy.

★ If your mud pie is a dark brown and keeps its basic mud-pie shape, yet it's kind of loose and crumbly, congratulations! Your soil is loam, the best garden soil around!

Not many people have loam, though, so don't worry. There are ways to make any soil nice and loamy. Keep reading.

LOAM, SWEET LOAM: THE PERFECT SOIL MIX

Loam is a rich, dark, chocolate color. It's light to the touch — almost fluffy — and it smells woodsy and good.

The secret of loam is compost: Any soil can become loamy with compost added to it. Compost makes clay soil lighter and easier to work with. It makes sandy soil better at holding water. Compost adds food to all soil.

COMPOST: THE MIRACLE WORKER

Compost is a kind of miracle worker, because it makes any soil healthy. Anything from the plant world can go into compost. That means coffee grounds, banana peels, egg shells, apple cores, walnut shells, carrot shreds — even pencil shavings! Making compost is so easy that if you follow a few simple rules, there's no way to go wrong. You can even make it in the great indoors!

Making indoor compost: To find out how Mother Nature turns garbage into compost, put a quart (or liter) of fruit or vegetable scraps in a clear plastic bag, and add a couple of hand-fuls of soil. Tie the bag shut with a twist tie. If you have a piece of plain charcoal — not the kind that's been soaked in lighter fluid — toss it in, too, to keep your compost smelling good.

Every few days or so, open the bag and stir it around. In about three weeks, you'll find that the bag of yucky old garbage has become a bag of sweet-smelling compost to sprinkle around your plants.

Sprinkle that compost around your houseplants and they will be very happy!

AN OUTDOOR COMPOST HEAP

Ask any gardener: You can never have enough of this rich, dark stuff! Compost does a kind of disappearing act! If you put lots of food scraps, weeds, grass clippings, and fallen leaves into the heap, they "cook" down to a small amount.

For best results, an outdoor compost heap needs to be at least one yard (one meter) high and one yard (one meter) wide. (Smaller heaps will work, but they take more time.)

THE SWEET SMELL OF SUCCESS

Your compost pile will smell woodsy and sweet, not rotten, if you follow these simple rules:

1 Make sure the heap has air. Give it a stir every now and then with a long stick.

2 The heap should be moist, but not wet. In a dry spell, you'll want to sprinkle it thoroughly with water. (If you are using the garbage can method, saw off the bottom.)

3 Cover the bin with a lid or with a layer of soil or peat moss to avoid pesky fruit flies. (Fruit flies are a nuisance, but they don't bite.)

NEAT HEAP

MAKE A SIMPLE OUTDOOR COMPOST BIN

You don't have to be a carpenter to make a compost bin. Any container that allows air and water into the heap will do.

The garbage bag method: Some people gather fall leaves in large garbage bags, add some soil, and then poke a few holes in the bags. As the bags sit behind bushes for a couple of years, the leaves gradually turn into compost. This is a lazy way to make compost, but it works.

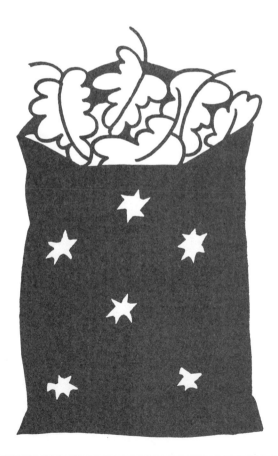

The garbage can method: You can also use an old garbage can with holes in it, or any kind of old container. An old wicker laundry basket makes a stylish compost bin, but remember, the wicker will rot in a year or so and become part of the compost!

A chicken wire bin: The simplest of compost bins is a circle made from chicken wire. Form the wire into a circle, and fill the circle with compost material, like grass clippings, old leaves, and food scraps. When the compost is dark and rich, like chocolate cake crumbs, remove the wire, and begin a new heap.

TREAT EARTHWORMS WITH RESPECT!

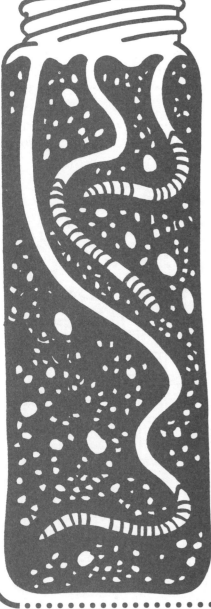

At this very moment, trillions of earthworms are out there, making our gardens healthy and green.

If you dig in dark soil, chances are you will soon come across an earthworm. Say hello and treat it with respect! People need earthworms, ever pushing through the soil, chomping as they go. The stuff their bodies get rid of as waste, called *castings*, is a valuable food for plant roots. It may not sound like an exciting life to us, but for a worm, the biggest thrill on earth is creating compost!

A closer look: To inspect a worm, have a soil-filled clear plastic or glass jar ready. Have the worm crawl onto a dark piece of paper. If you want to hold it, do so gently. (Never pick up a worm by pinching it.)

When it's in your hand or on paper, look at it with a magnifying glass. You'll see lots of little rings, which are the muscles that help the worm plow through soil. On its underside, look for the tiny "feet" that grip the soil. On one end, you'll find an "eye" that does the "sensing." Watch the worm try to find its way home with that eye.

Worms need to be in dark, moist soil so *please don't keep your worm out in the open for more than a minute or two*. After you've looked it over, drop the worm in the jar and watch what it does. Down, down, down it goes.

When it's time to return your worm to Mother Earth, tell it "thanks!" A worm may be lowly, but it's one of Nature's most important workers.

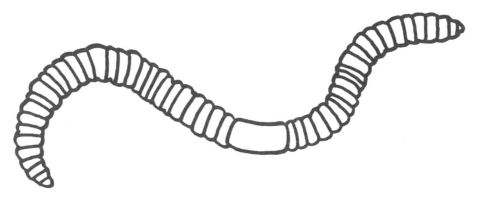

KEEP PET WORMS IN AN INDOOR COMPOST BIN

Some earth-friendly people keep worms under the sink or in a closet. These slinky pets are quiet and out of the way as they chomp kitchen garbage to make you free plant food.

The bin does not smell, and the worms will not want to escape. Here's how to make a comfy home for earthworms:

YOU'LL NEED:

A container with a lid, or a covered box at least 10" (24 cm) deep

Shredded newspapers (bedding for the worms)

Soil to start the bin

Bunch of earthworms

Steady supply of moist kitchen scraps

Put about three inches (7.5 cm) of shredded newspaper on the bottom of the box, and fill the box halfway up with soil, leaving room for air. Toss in the worms and say, "Bye," because the moment they hit the soil, the worms will dig in.

Mix in the fruit and vegetable scraps with dirt. Every day or so, mix in a clump of food scraps. Cover with dirt. Keep an old chopstick in the bin to give the compost a stir every now and then.

Every few weeks, take out the fresh compost for your houseplants, and add new bedding for those hard-working worms. They deserve it for all the good they do!

DO NOT DISTURB! WORMS AT WORK

MUSCLE POWER!

If you are using sheer muscle power, get as many people as you can to help, especially a grown-up or two. If you have a dog who likes to dig, find a way to get it on the job! Your goal is to dig at least ten inches (24 cm) deep.

It's a big job! But while you work, think of the beautiful bouquets and tasty salads you'll enjoy! Those kinds of thoughts make work go faster!

Save your back: When you dig with a spade, keep your back straight and use your legs as much as possible. Bend your knees, not your back.

Take breaks, too, so you don't run out of steam before the job is done. Fruit juice and seltzer make a cool drink, and regular breaks will help you work harder for a longer time.

COMFY EARTH BEDS

Making a garden bed is harder than making your bed in the morning. In fact, when folks say gardening is hard work, preparing the soil is the part they mean! Still, the effort you put in here will pay off in a big, beautiful way as your garden grows.

BUST THOSE CLODS!

When you first turn it over, the soil will be clumpy and lumpy. That's where your trusty hoe comes in. Chop those clumps, and bust those clods!

Once you've busted the clods, it's time to fluff up the soil. Peat moss is light and wonderful stuff to toss in, along with as much compost as you have. Good garden soil also needs a healthy dose of dried *manure* (man-OOR), or dried animal droppings. Manure adds all sorts of nutrients to the soil — the food that plant roots need.

The final result should be dark brown or black soil that looks like crumbly, chocolate cake. What a treat for your plants!

GROW A FAST-FOOD SALAD

If you're hungry and in a hurry, try planting a fast-food salad of red and white radishes and spring greens. Your salad will be ready to eat in just three weeks — that's super-speedy in gardening time!

And think about this: Fast-food gardening comes with a prize that's much more valuable than a plastic toy: It's the gift of patience! That gift lasts forever.

HERE WE GO!

Outies begin here; Innies, check out page 50.

Lettuce: Choose leaf or oakleaf lettuce for growing speed.

Radishes: Bright red radishes are the absolute fastest growing veggie. For fast results, sprout the seeds indoors and transplant as soon as you can. They add pizzazz to any salad, too.

Spinach: Plant the seeds outdoors as soon as the danger of frost is past. Speedy spinach likes cool weather more than most plants.

Herbs: Add some zest to your salad bowl, and a pretty place in you garden, too. Snip herbs as they grow to add lots of flavor to your salad. (See "Herbs for Oomph!" page 115 – 124.)

BRIGHT GREEN THUMB

Harvesting Your Fast-Food Greens

Harvest salad greens by giving them a crew cut. When you have a bunch of tasty lettuce leaves, cut them off, leaving an inch or two (about 4 to 5 cm) of green. The plant will grow back a couple more times, giving you more to eat!

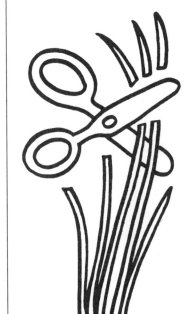

MIXED GREENS TO GO

Lettuce comes in lots of different styles and tastes, like curly or straight, crispy or smooth. Romaine lettuce is kind of tall (for lettuce, that is) and stately, while salad bowl lettuce looks like it has a curly permanent. Plant a few different kinds for an extra-delicious mixed green salad!

MARKERS FOR THE GARDEN

Once a seed goes into the ground, it's easy to forget what you planted and where you planted it! To make colorful, waterproof plant markers, you'll need wire hangers and a few clear, plastic protective sheets, the kind used to hold baseball cards or photos.

1 Ask a grown-up to help you snip the hangers with a wire cutter and uncurl the end with pliers. Form each wire piece into a U-shape.

2 Cut out one of the plastic protective pockets, and slip the empty seed package inside. If you don't have a seed package, draw a picture of the plant you have planted.

3 Place this over the ends of the hanger for the coolest markers any garden has ever seen!

THE EASIEST GARDEN MARKER

Draw a picture or write the name of what you've planted on a paint stirrer in waterproof paint. Your local paint store will probably give you some stirrers for free if you don't have any on hand. (Innies can use tongue depressors or craft sticks.)

CUT WIRE HANGER INTO SECTIONS

BEND SECTIONS INTO U-SHAPES

CARROT SEED

INSERT SEED PACKET INTO PLASTIC POCKET

CARROT SEED

SLIP OVER HANGER SECTION

corn

peas

MAKE A SCARECROW!

Scarecrows have been chasing away birds from gardens for hundreds of years. Late winter, before you plant your garden, is the perfect time to create a scarecrow. Ask some friends to help you create a scarecrow that is truly one-of-a-kind.

YOU'LL NEED:

2 sticks, one longer than the other. (Broomsticks or old fence slats are perfect.)

Old clothing, including hats, scarves

Aluminum pie pans to make jangling bracelets, and jingle-bell belts.

Stuffing (Hay is traditional, but lint from the dryer works well, too.)

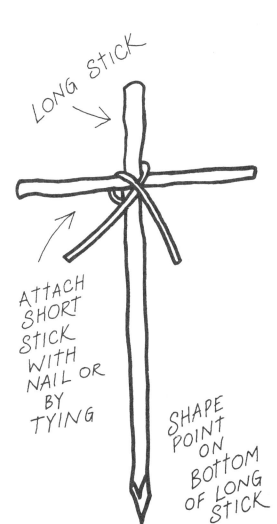

LONG STICK

ATTACH SHORT STICK WITH NAIL OR BY TYING

SHAPE POINT ON BOTTOM OF LONG STICK

STUFF OLD PILLOWCASE WITH STRAW

SEW ON BUTTONS FOR EYES AND NOSE

DRAW MOUTH

DRESS UP YOUR SCARECROW

PUSH POINTED END OF STICK INTO GROUND

The skeleton: Ask a grown-up to supervise as you whittle the long stick to a point. To create "shoulders," attach the shorter stick crosswise with nails or by tying.

Face and head: Stuff an old pillowcase and tie to the top of the broomstick. Sew on two big button eyes, paint a nose and mouth, and watch the crows zoom away! Or, try a clown face or mask creation.

The perfect outfit: When it comes to clothes for your scarecrow, anything goes, as long as the outfit is bold and old. Brightly colored hats and pocketbooks swinging in the breeze add to the fun — oops, we mean the fright — of these scary creatures!

SPRING SALAD FOR INDOOR GARDENERS

Yes! It can be done! You may not be able to produce what a forty-acre field does, but your indoor produce is extra-satisfying. It's great to nibble a salad you grew yourself on the windowsill.

WHAT IT TAKES

Pots deep enough for healthy roots, prepared soil, water, and sunlight are all you need to grow food in the Great Indoors.

Choose seeds of the smaller varieties, like Tom Thumb carrots, or Bibb lettuce. These don't need the growing space of their larger cousins.

Plant and water as you would any seeds (see page 32).

Cover the pots with clear plastic or a homemade greenhouse (page 35).

When your seeds turn into seedlings move them to the sunniest place in the house. We knew an indoor gardener who had a "rolling farm." It was a piece of plywood on a wagon that she moved from window to window to catch the most sun. That wagon produced some mighty fine salad after a few weeks!

BRIGHT GREEN THUMB

Not Enough Sun? Try A Grow Light!

A grow light is a special light bulb sold in gardening supply shops that gives off all the rays your plants will need to grow and produce. They're not expensive and are easy to rig up with a little help from a grown-up.

INNIES' SPRING SALAD

Try these varieties for small size but big taste:

Sweet banana peppers: These are shaped like little bananas. Harvest them when they turn red for a sweet, tangy treat.

Champion radishes: These cherry-red radishes will be mild and tender if you pick them early. Plant matures in just 28 days.

Mighty Midget peas: The vines are just 6 inches (15 cm) short, but these peas are long on taste!

Carrots: Short 'n' Sweet, Little Finger, Tiny Sweet, or Tom Thumb are great varieties for growing indoors. Crisp and delicious!

Patio Pik cucumbers: The vine is about 5 inches (12.5 cm) long. Remember, only one cucumber to a pot, though.

Lettuce: Varieties like Tom Thumb, Bibb, and Oakleaf lettuce don't mind being crowded, so try two heads to a pot. Their leaves are tender and tasty. Pick a few leaves every night for fresh salad eating.

Cherry tomatoes: Cherry tomatoes are good for container growing, if you get lots of sun. If your space is really small, try the Microtom tomato that grows just 6 inches (15 cm) high but produces about 30 little tomatoes!

WIGGLE, WATER, AND FEED YOUR INDOOR FARM

Feed your plants with fertilizer — once when they are seedlings, and again when they flower. Remember, though: Too much fertilizer is as bad as not enough.

As for watering, use the wiggly-finger test to see when to water and when to hold off. If the soil is dry, give your plants a drink.

HARVESTING YOUR INDOOR PRODUCE

Your indoor produce is cause for a celebration. The food you grow will be worth making a fuss over. Even if the harvest isn't exactly bountiful, it will be beautiful.

Radish Rosettes

Cut radishes into stylish rosettes to add elegance to your salad. Start by getting a grown-up's permission to use a small paring knife. Slice "petals" into the radishes by making four or five slash cuts around the bulb and gently tugging on them. These will resemble the outer petals of a rose. Finish by cutting three or four "petals" in the center of the radish.

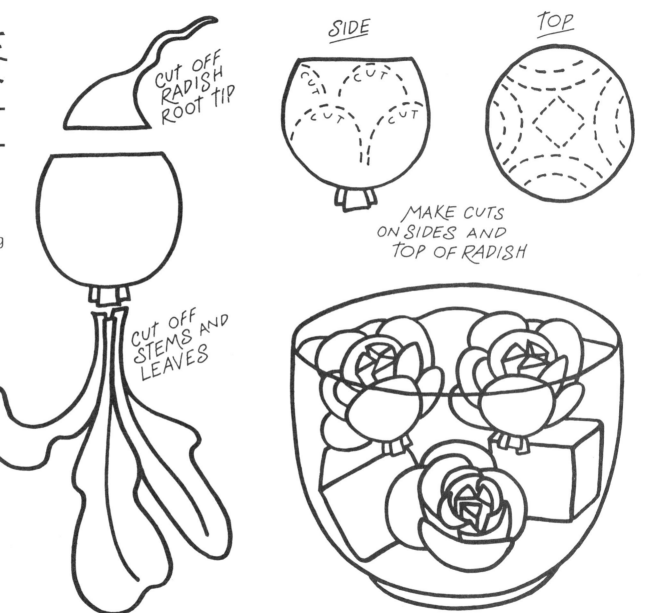

CUT OFF RADISH ROOT TIP

CUT OFF STEMS AND LEAVES

SIDE

TOP

MAKE CUTS ON SIDES AND TOP OF RADISH

SOAK ROSETTES IN ICE WATER UNTIL PETALS OPEN

FOOD FUN

Fifi's French Salad Dressing

YOU'LL NEED:

1/2 cup (125 ml) oil

1/2 cup (125 ml) wine vinegar

2 tablespoons (25 ml) ketchup

1/2 teaspoon (2 ml) dry mustard

1/2 teaspoon (2 ml) salt

1/2 teaspoon (2 ml) paprika

1/8 teaspoon (.5 ml) black or white pepper

Put the ingredients in a bowl, and shake, shake, shake!

CRAN-RASP SALAD DRESSING

This dressing adds fruity zest to any salad. Mix a can of raspberry-cranberry sauce and a little water in a blender for two minutes. Pour over your spring greens.

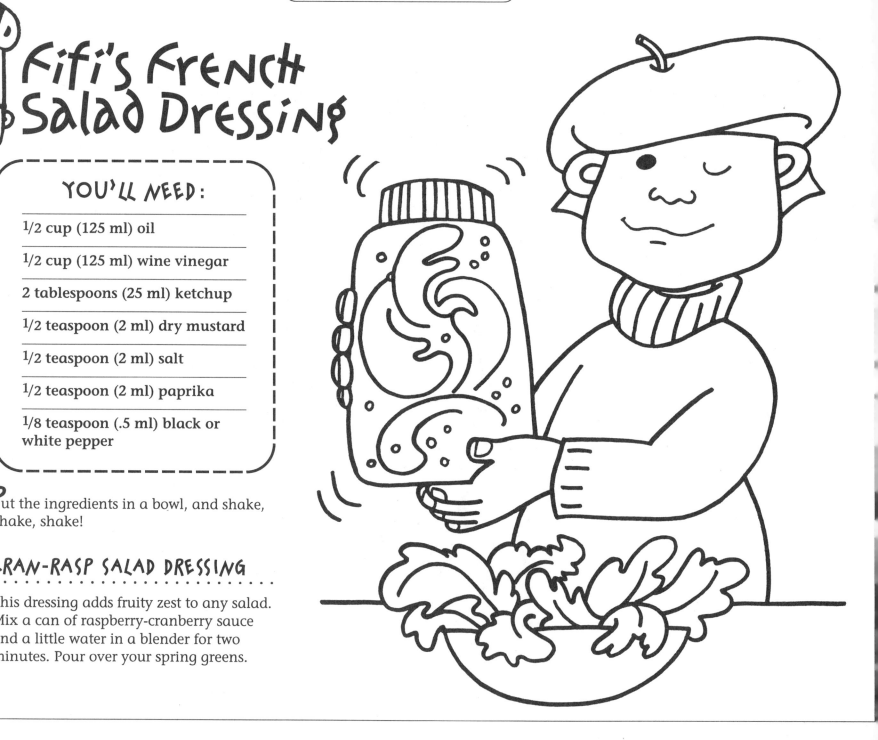

MUNCH! CRUNCH! GROW YOUR LUNCH!

Plant a seed and harvest a carrot, cucumber, some potatoes or beans. It doesn't matter if you have a field out back or a sunny apartment windowsill. You can grow a mini-farm that will pay off in tasty rewards!

PLOTTING A MINI-FARM

(Innies, see page 50.)
How will you choose what to grow? Ask yourself: What do you and your family like to eat? Fresh beans? Juicy tomatoes? Cool cukes? Crunchy carrots? Leafy lettuce?

   If you have a patch of land about 2 square yards (2 square meters), you can grow one or two plants of each! (Don't worry, Innies. Good things to eat can be grown in pots, too. See page 50.)

Do a survey: Ask each person in your family to write down their five favorite vegetables. Collect their answers and look for veggies that made it to more than one list. (Write a list of your own, and let it count double, because you're the farmer!)

   Plot your design with colored markers (see page 47). Use a ruler to create the borders of your garden and draw circles and oblongs to stand for the plants you want to grow.

   Remember, plants grow! That teeny speck of a lettuce seed can grow into something the size of a beach ball, so leave space for that future growth!

CATNIP

LUCY

Garden Salsa

YOU'LL NEED:

1 tablespoon (15 ml) chopped onion

1 large or 2 medium tomatoes

4 green chili peppers

1 1/2 tablespoons (22.5 ml) chopped parsley or cilantro

1 teaspoon (5 ml) lime or lemon juice

For spicy salsa, add 2 chopped jalapeno peppers. If you grow some parsley or cilantro in your herb garden (see page 116), add a generous tablespoon of each.

Ask a grown-up to help you chop all the ingredients that can be chopped (use a blender if you want). Add the rest of the ingredients and mix together.

Let the salsa sit for a few minutes until the flavors all blend. Serve right away with vegetable sticks or corn chips.

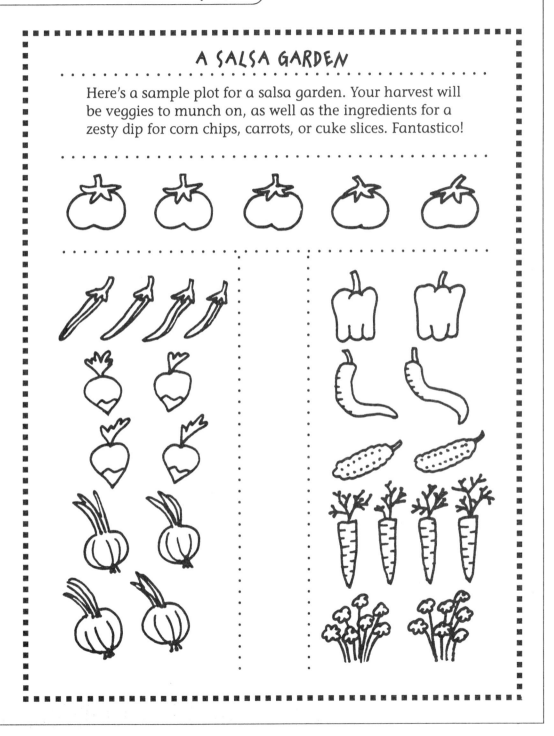

A SALSA GARDEN

Here's a sample plot for a salsa garden. Your harvest will be veggies to munch on, as well as the ingredients for a zesty dip for corn chips, carrots, or cuke slices. Fantastico!

NATIVE AMERICAN GARDEN GREATS

THE THREE SISTERS: CORN, BEANS, AND SQUASH

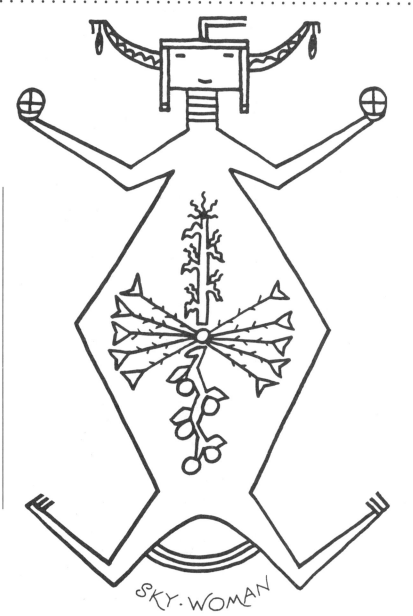

SKY·WOMAN

If you have a sunny garden, you can plant the foods that native people call the Three Sisters — corn, beans, and summer squash. The Iroquois believe that these foods are a gift from the goddess, Sky Woman, who created the first people. In Iroquois legend, Sky Woman came from heaven, created people, and gave them the Three Sisters to keep them happy and healthy.

When the Three Sisters are grown together, their roots nourish each other by sending out compatible nutrients! Sky Woman was very wise — the Iroquois people knew instinctively what science took much longer to find out!

Sky Woman was an efficiency expert, too! Growing the Three Sisters doesn't take a lot of room or trouble, because the beans climb up the corn stalks, and the squash keeps the ground below shaded and free of weeds. Simply create a little hill of prepared soil in one sunny square yard (square meter) to grow two corn plants, six pole bean plants, and one squash plant. (Plant any kind of bean.)

FOOD FUN

Ogonsaganonda

When the corn is ready to eat, make ogonsaganonda, a fresh, delicious succotash.

YOU'LL NEED:

2 cups (500 ml) fresh corn kernels

3 cups (750 ml) beans (any kind — mix and match!)

1 or 2 summer squash — cut in small pieces

1 cup (250 ml) water or, better yet, vegetable broth

3 tablespoons (40 ml) butter or vegetable oil

1 small onion cut in small pieces (optional)

1 sweet red pepper cut in small pieces (optional)

Salt to taste (optional)

1 Ask a grown-up to melt the butter or heat the oil in a saucepan. Add pepper and onion if you are using them. Heat for 5 minutes, gently stirring.

2 Add the other ingredients. Cover tightly and simmer on low heat for 20 minutes. Then drain carefully.

3 Serve in a big bowl. Top with a squash blossom, if you have one. Talk about the things nature provides for us.

A GREENER WORLD

Using All of It

Corn is one of those great crops that you can eat fresh, frozen, or dried, and you can use the husks, too. Look in any craft book for directions on making a cornhusk doll, or make a harvest cornhusk wreath by tying dried strips of husk onto a cardboard wreath shape. Don't forget to put the silk and those munched-on cobs into your compost bin for a greener world.

THANK YOU, AMERICAN INDIANS!

Think about this: The Native Americans of North and South America gave us so many important foods that we would be very hungry if we had to try to go without them today.

Every one of these foods was first discovered, and then generously shared, by the native people of the Americas! How many of these foods are your favorites to eat for dinner?

Potatoes

Peanuts

Beans

Tomatoes

Pineapples

Chocolate and cocoa

Shrimp, Lobster

Corn

Strawberries

Peppers

Maple syrup and sugar

Vanilla

Wild rice

Pumpkins

Squash

Sunflower seeds

Plums

Avocados

Tapioca

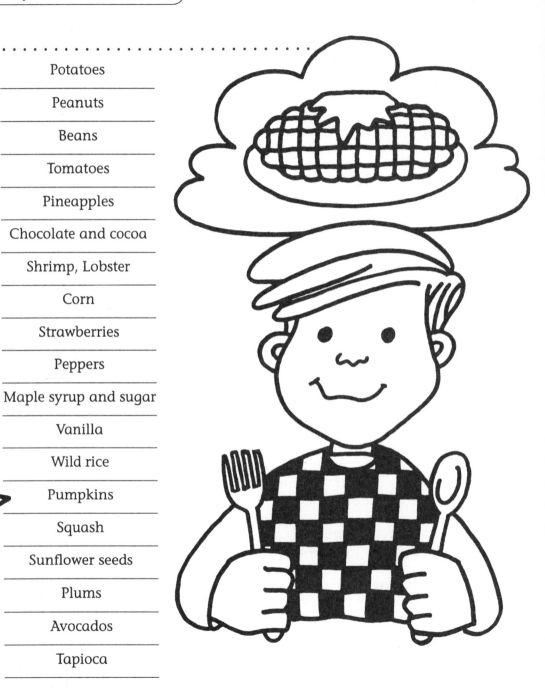

CELEBRATE!

Harvests 'Round the World

In the United States, people celebrate a harvest festival in November called Thanksgiving. Other cultures have harvest festivals, too. In Israel, they celebrate Succoth. Everyone builds little booths outdoors, with make-shift wooden walls. There's no ceiling in the "succah" — it's open to the sky and the stars. The walls are decorated with boughs, branches, and the fruits of the harvest. The family gathers there to eat the fruit of their labor. Guests are welcome to share in the joy and the bounty.

Every culture has its own harvest-celebrating traditions. Ask the grown-ups in your family which country or countries your ancestors are from, and how people celebrate the harvest there.

TOO MANY ZUCCHINI?

Zucchini — like their cousins, summer squash — are super growers, and you may get more than you've bargained for! Plant two or three zucchini or summer squash seeds or seedlings, but once they take off, leave only the one or two healthiest plants. Even then, you'll be giving zucchini to your friends and neighbors, as you share Mother Nature's generosity!

Zucchini and summer squash are best when they are picked while still small — only about five inches long. Slice them to add to salads, brush with flavored oil and put on the grill, or cut into "sticks" to dip in guacamole (see page 13). Grate the ones that get too big and bake zucchini bread, or scoop them out and fill with your favorite fillings.

Zucchini Drop Cookies

There isn't a better-tasting solution to the too-many-zucchini problem than this one!

YOU'LL NEED:

2 cups (500 ml) flour

1 cup (250 ml) grated zucchini

1 teaspoon (5 ml) baking soda

3/4 cup (175 ml) sugar

1/2 cup (125 ml) butter

1 egg

1/2 teaspoon (2 ml) cinnamon

1/2 teaspoon (2 ml) ground cloves

1 cup (250 ml) raisins

1 cup (250 ml) chopped nuts

Mix everything together and drop by spoonfuls onto a greased cookie sheet. Bake for 12 to 15 minutes at 375° F. (190 ° C) Yum!

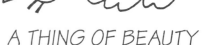

P.S.!

A THING OF BEAUTY

By the way, squash blossoms are not only beautiful to look at, they are very tasty to eat! And while we are on the subject of edible blossoms, nasturtiums can add more than color to your salad; they add a tangy, peppery flavor, too! (See note, page 67.)

BEANS! BEANS! BEANS!

They've been used for casting votes. They've been thought of as the symbol of life. They say a fellow named Jack once climbed one's vine up into the sky!

They can be made into milk, flour, hamburgers, or pancakes. Scientists say they can help feed the whole world! The ancient Egyptians ate them. Cowboys ate them. You and I eat them today!

We're talking about beans and peas, whose official name is legumes (LEG-yoomz). They are easy to grow and packed with food power. No wonder people have eaten them since 9700 B.C., when, scientists tell us, they were growing in Thailand!

BEANS IN YOUR GARDEN

Planting beans makes a lot of sense because each bean plant produces lots and lots of beans. You can plant bush beans that grow in bushes, or pole beans that like to climb up poles and fences. You can even plant trick beans that grow purple but turn bright green when you toss them into hot water!

POLE BEANS

TRICK BEANS

BUSH BEANS

Science sense

How Powerful Are They?

Plaster is the stuff that walls are made of — but it's no match for a bean seed! To get an idea of the power packed into a bean seed, in an old coffee can, mix two cups of plaster of Paris with a little water, until the plaster is like thick cream.

Now, "plant" three or four bean seeds under the surface. When the plaster dries it will be as hard as a rock. You won't see the bean seeds inside. Keep the plaster moist by sprinkling water on it every day.

In a few days, the plaster will break up like a sidewalk in an earthquake! That's pure bean seed power!

COFFEE ← CAN

← BEANS

← PLASTER

A BEAN-POLE TEPEE

Do you like secret places that are just big enough to fit you and maybe a friend? Do you like to munch on green beans fresh off the vine? If you said yes to these questions, then growing a bean-pole tepee is for you!

YOU'LL NEED:

Seeds or seedlings of pole (runner) beans and nasturtium flowers

6 bamboo poles (or broom sticks, or tall straight branches)

Brightly colored cloth strips

Heavy nylon string

You may want to start your bean plants indoors, so that you will have more time to enjoy the tepee (see page 33).

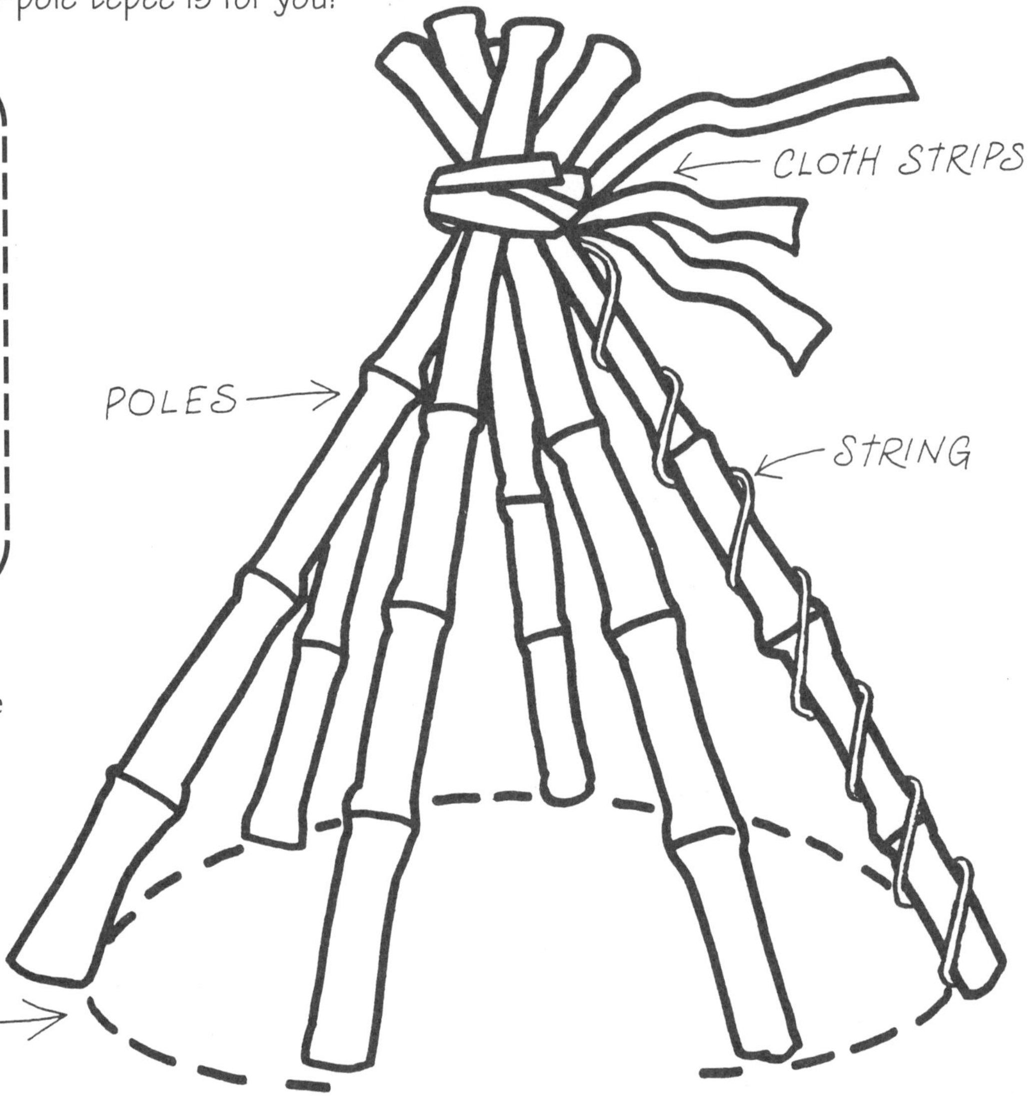

← CLOTH STRIPS

POLES →

← STRING

"C" SHAPE →

The tepee is made from bamboo poles, or any other poles that are at least six feet (2 meters) tall — the taller the better! Place your tepee where it will get lots of sun.

Prepare the soil (see page 39), and stick the poles firmly into the ground in the shape of the letter C. The opening will be the "door" of your tepee. Tie the tops of the poles with strips of brightly colored cloth to help keep hungry birds away.

Then, wind thick nylon string around each pole, from top to bottom. Scatter shade-loving grass seed for the floor of the tepee.

Plant one or two runner bean seeds near each pole. Sprinkle nasturtium seeds outside the tepee. Before you know it, your tepee will be a home away from home. And just think, the flowery "wallpaper" is alive and ready for nibbling whenever you get hungry!

Note: Not all flowers are for eating, of course. Most are for looking at and smelling. Nasturtiums and squash blossoms can be eaten, but *always ask a grown-up before eating any flowers.*

Remember: Some flowers are poisonous.

HOMEGROWN 'TATERS!

Call them potatoes, taters, or just plain spuds. Eat them mashed, baked, boiled, diced, home-fried, hash-browned, French-fried, in salads, or as chips!

Potatoes are a true wonder food, packed with vitamins and minerals for good health and energy. No wonder potatoes are the most widely grown and eaten vegetable in the entire world!

P.S.!

A GRUBBY LUMP WORTH MORE THAN GOLD

When the Spanish explorers arrived in South America back in the 1500s, they were searching for gold and silver treasure. Little did they realize that the lumpy "patatas" that the native people ate would one day be worth far more than all the gold and silver in the world! Today's global potato crop takes in over $100 billion a year!

THE EYES HAVE IT

Planting potatoes is easy if you've got a sunny place in the backyard, or a large pot out on the deck or stoop. All you need is a potato! (Organic potatoes, ones that haven't been sprayed with artificial chemicals, are the best seed potatoes and also are the best for eating.)

The seeds of the potato are in the lumpy part we call the "eyes." Although these bumps may seem like imperfections, they are really nature's way of making more potatoes.

Cut the seed potato into four pieces, making sure each piece has an eye. Plant the pieces about four inches (10 cm) deep. Water and wait.

Soon, a green sprout will appear and grow into a leafy plant that will produce flowers with little yellow dots. Let the flowers bloom and fade. Keep watering and waiting.

Under the ground, potatoes are forming as tubers that grow on the roots of the plant. Pull up the plant at the end of the season, when frost comes. Happy eating!

FOOD FUN — Clothed or . . . Not!

To make mashed potatoes, scrub, cut, and boil your spuds until they are soft. Have a grown-up drain the water from the pot, get a masher or big fork, and go to work! Mash in a dollop of butter, a little milk, and a dash of salt.

We mash potatoes with the skins on at our house, because we like the earthy taste and the extra vitamins we get that way. Some people say, "You eat potatoes with the skins on?" To them, we say, "You eat potatoes naked?"

DO THE MASHED POTATO!

Back in the 1960s there was a song and dance called "The Mashed Potato." Find some grown-ups who were teens back then and ask them to sing it for you — or check it out at an "oldies" music shop. It's kind of silly, but a lot of fun.

To dance the Mashed Potato, press the balls of your feet down one at a time as you move your heels from side to side — as if you were squishing potatoes with your toes!

CELEBRATE!

Real Potato Chips

What's a party without potato chips? You've eaten them from a bag, but how about trying potato chips fresh from your oven? They're easy to make, and taste terrific!

Ask a grown-up to slice the potatoes thinly. Oil a cookie sheet; then spread out the potato slices like cookies. Wipe some oil on the tops of the slices and bake in a hot oven until the potatoes are brownish and crispy. Salt to taste.

Bet you can't eat just one!

HURRAY FOR TOMATOES!

Science Sense

A True Tomato Story

In 1820, Robert Johnson stood on the courthouse steps of Salem, New Jersey, and shocked his neighbors by eating a big, red, ripe, juicy tomato. The people who watched were horrified! Everybody back then knew that tomatoes were deadly poisonous!

Mr. Johnson ate not one, but a whole pailful of tomatoes. Then, with a lively spring in his step, he walked down the stairs, got in his horse-drawn buggy, and drove off.

Since then, people have been eating tomatoes by the bushelful — and no one has ever gotten sick from a tomato as far as we know! Thank you, Robert Johnson, for clearing up a misunderstanding about one of our favorite foods!

GROWING TOMATOES

You'll need hours of sun and rich, loose soil to grow tomatoes whether you start them from seeds or from seedlings.

They may grow so big that they need to be staked, or tied to a pole. (Any long, straight stick will do.) Tie the stake to the stem with a long twist-tie, nylon string, or a strip of cloth.

Tomatoes get thirsty. Be sure to give them plenty of water. (Water the roots, not the leaves.)

Don't be bugged: Bugs love tomatoes as much as people do, so be sure to read up on getting rid of garden pests when you plant tomatoes (see "Trouble in Paradise," page 143).

Speecy, Spicy Tomato Sauce!

This recipe for tomato sauce is a real lollapalooza. In other words, it's awesome!

YOU'LL NEED:

Lots of tomatoes (12 to 20 — or use canned tomatoes)

Olive oil

Fresh basil, marjoram, or oregano, chopped (from your herb garden, of course)

2 large cans of tomato paste

Minced garlic, onion, and salt, to taste

Kidney beans, mushrooms, peppers, or zucchinis (optional)

Put a tablespoon of oil in a large pan and *sauté* (cook lightly) the garlic and onion, if you are using them. Cut the tomatoes into six pieces each and start simmering them, too. Keep the lid off so that the liquid cooks down. When the tomatoes are mushy, stir in the paste. That is the basic sauce.

Now, to make it speecy spicy, neecy nicey, start adding everything you can think of that might be good. How about a couple of handfuls of fresh herbs (much less if using dried herbs), a can of drained kidney beans, some sliced small zucchini or summer squash, or sliced peppers and mushrooms? What else sounds good?

Simmer together for 20 to 30 minutes. (Don't forget to stir!) Serve on thin spaghetti, with a loaf of crusty Italian or French bread.

Dee-lish!

TOMATO BOATS

For an easy, yummy lunch, slice off the top of a tomato and gently empty out the insides. Stuff tuna fish salad into the empty tomato shell, and serve with sliced cucumbers.

CUT

SCOOP OUT SEEDS AND PULP, THEN STUFF

Throw a Plot Luck Harvest Party

You have 25 samurai-sized zucchinis ready to pick, and tomatoes bursting out of your garden like firecrackers going off on the 4th of July. The beans may be coming out of your ears!

What do you do when your garden explodes with good things to eat?

Have a party — a pot luck — make that plot luck — party, for you, your neighbors, and friends.

Chances are, if your garden is overflowing, somebody down the road is having a bountiful harvest, too! What better way to celebrate all that success than by sharing?

A plot luck party doesn't cost much, because everyone brings a casserole, salad, or dessert.

The best place to have a plot luck party is outdoors, where all those delicious fruits and veggies came from in the first place. Get out the lawn chairs and old blankets. Because when the sun goes down and the stars come out, there's nothing like summertime stargazing with a bunch of people you like.

Patio Pumpkins

Jack Be Littles are pumpkins you can grow in a large pot on your deck. The vine will ramble about 8 to 12 feet (about 3 meters), but the pumpkins will be as cute as the pies you can bake from them! (Seed ordering, see page 37.)

MORE GARDEN GREATS

A SMILING PUMPKIN PATCH

Maybe it's their bright orange color, or their leaves that look like big green stars, or maybe it's the super energy they give our bodies. When you grow a pumpkin patch, you'll also grow a smile!

Pumpkins need a lot of room because they grow on rambling vines. Leave at least one square yard (meter) for each plant.

Make a hill of healthy garden soil and plant 3 to 4 pumpkin seeds on top. After they sprout, choose the strongest plant to keep growing, and cut down the others.

Your vine will creep and wander over the ground. Then big flowers will appear. Each of these flowers will develop into a pumpkin!

For bigger pumpkins, snip off some of the flowers on each vine. Your pumpkin plant will put all its effort into the flowers that are left!

SEED

AN AUTOGRAPHED PUMPKIN

You can create a special pumpkin — signed by you! Write your name in a pumpkin when it is still small and green. Don't press too hard, but do make an indentation. As the pumpkin grows, so will your name! If you have a big pumpkin patch, why not make an autographed pumpkin for every family on your street or everyone in your class next fall.

PICKLE IN A BOTTLE

Here's a fun gift to make — a big pickle in a little bottle. How will the person get the pickle out of the bottle? That's the trick! But here is the secret of getting it inside:

Place a tiny baby cuke that's still growing on the vine inside a small glass jar. Set the jar on the soil so the cuke can continue to grow. Cover the bottle with a few leaves to keep it from the direct sunlight.

The bottle acts like a greenhouse, and soon the cuke will fill it up completely! Snip and give!

COOL CUKES

There's certainly nothing like a cold, crisp cuke on a hot day. A plate of them makes a great meal in itself! Cucumbers grow along the ground on vines that like to take over your garden, so they need plenty of room. Their flowers of brilliant sunshine yellow yield lots of cucumbers that are best picked at four or five inches (10–12 cm) long.

Avoid a cuke duke-it-out!: Growing cukes is easy as long as you know this secret: Cucumbers are jealous of other cucumbers! If one cuke plant is too close to another, each will send out special chemicals designed to keep the other plant small! To avoid this sibling rivalry, make sure each cuke has enough "personal space." Plant them at least 12 inches (or 40 cm) apart.

CAPTIVATING CARROTS

With their lacy green tops, carrots are pretty plants in the garden. They like sandy soil best, but they'll grow in any good garden soil that is not too clayey or rocky. (Rocks in the soil make L-shaped carrots!)

After you've eaten them, grow some carrot tops as a pretty houseplant! (See page 15.)

FOOD FUN Cold Carrot Soup

Bright orange soup? Wait till you taste it! The ingredients include butter, sliced carrots, fresh ginger, cinnamon, orange juice, lemon juice, milk, chopped onion, and vanilla. Try it for supper on a hot summer night.

1 Sauté (lightly cook) 2 tablespoons (25 ml) of butter, a little chopped onion, and a teaspoon (5 ml) of fresh ginger.

2 Cook the carrots until they are tender, then add them to the sauté for 3 to 4 minutes. Cook for 5 more minutes and then let it cool.

3 Add a cup (250 ml) of orange juice, a cup (250 ml) of milk, 2 tablespoons (25 ml) of lemon juice, a dash of vanilla, and a teaspoon (5 ml) of cinnamon. Blend all together in a blender or food processor.

Serve cold. Yum!

CELEBRATE!

A Rotten-Vegetable Hoedown!

Unpicked, overripe tomatoes and squash get squishy after a while. Just put on your boots and ask a couple of friends to help you mush and mash the overripe veggies! You'll be composting the veggies into the soil, making it richer for the next season.

Try singing while you stomp! And if you have a friend who can play an instrument, have him or her join in, too! Yee-haw!

BRILLIANT BOUQUETS!

Flowers everywhere! On the table! On the bureau! In a vase on a desk! Bursting, bright, bubbling bunches of flowers that make you smile just looking at them!

When flowers bloom, it's as if Mother Nature is winking and saying "Hi!" You don't need a giant-sized field to grow a bouquet — just one square yard (meter) will give lots of flowers, if you grow the right kind.

PLANNING A BOUQUET GARDEN

WHAT'S YOUR STYLE?

It doesn't matter much which way you grow them — flowers are beautiful every which way! But we wonder what your flower garden will be like...

How do you keep your Legos™?: Some naturally neat and orderly kids — yes, they do exist — grow their flowers by height. These are the kids who keep their Legos™ organized by size in separate containers, and always put their pencils back in the box.

They put tallest plants in the back, middle-sized plants in the middle, and shorter plants in the front of the garden. That type of design is very popular in England, where gardening is practically the national pastime!

How did you eat your peas?: Some kids make small plots (or groups of pots), with just one kind of flower inside each space. These are the kids who, when they were babies, used to wail if one little pea touched their mashed potatoes. Growing flowers in individual patches is a fine way to grow flowers, though, no matter what you were like as a baby.

What does your closet look like?: Other kids like to mix and match their flowers, making a colorful jumble of this and that. They scatter their seeds on a fresh bed of soil, willy-nilly style. These are the kids whose closets are all...well, you get the idea! In a mixed-flower garden, planting the seeds is like tossing confetti!

THE BEST BOUQUET FLOWERS FROM A TO Z

Here's a list of flowers that are perfect for bouquets. Prepare the soil (see page 39) and follow your sun map (see page 17). These flowers are all easy to grow, and best of all, the more you cut them, the more they bloom, bloom, bloom!

Asters (small, medium, or tall)

Coreopsis (tickseed) (medium)

Larkspur (medium to tall)

Pansies (small)

Baby's-breath (tall)

Cornflowers (medium)

Tulips (medium to tall)

Bachelor's Buttons (medium)

Daisies (medium to tall)

Marigolds (small to medium)

Violets (small)

Mums (medium)

Zinnias (medium to tall)

CELEBRATE!

A House of Flowers

You can make a house of hollyhocks, sunflowers, delphiniums, or even corn! These plants are all very tall and can serve as walls. Just plant in a box shape. When the plants grow up, they will become a great place to play. Invite a friend, too. But remember: If you build your house of corn, don't tell secrets inside it. The corn has ears!

Celebrate!

A Birthday Chair

You can make a "birthday chair" for someone special — as they do in the Baltic country of Lithuania — by attaching flowers and ribbons to the top of a kitchen chair.

Start with little bunches of flowers tied with twist ties. Lightly tape them onto the chair, and then wind a thick ribbon to cover the wires. The birthday person will feel like real royalty when he or she sits on the specially created chair!

PAINT YOUR GARDEN

Artists have been drawing and painting flowers since time began. Claude Monet won world fame as a painter, but he often claimed that his gardens were his greatest creations. He used his garden as a source of inspiration for his art. The gigantic paintings of water lilies he grew are world famous!

A work of art is a wonderful way to remember the good times you spend in your garden. Try doing a watercolor of what you think your flower garden will look like. Then, when your garden is in full bloom, do another watercolor of the way it really came out!

Were they mostly similar, or amazingly different? Either way, you've imagined, designed, and helped make something beautiful!

AMAZING ANNUALS

Flowers that grow and bloom for just one season are called *annuals* (ANN-you-als). Flowers that come up year after year are called *perennials* (per-EN-ee-als). Plant some of each for a great, blooming garden! (Innies, check out page 89.)

AND THE WINNERS ARE . . . .

These popular annuals are a snap to grow (especially, the snapdragons). Once you've prepared good soil for them, all they'll need is a little water now and then.

The envelope, please....

Petunias: Pretty petunia has been pleasing people for years, and she is one star whose charm never fades. She is a smash in "Any Sunny Spot," and "Revenge of the Deadheads."

Zinnias: Bold and dramatic, this star of the garden is featured in three hits! "The Bouquet," "Making Dyes," and "Come Close to Me," the touching story of her relationship with a butterfly.

Marigolds: Miniature or full-grown, this flower gets Best Supporting Performer for its role in "Keeping Pests Away," and "Helping Tomatoes."

Sweet alyssum: This low-growing star with white or purple flowers made his reputation in "An Annual On the Edge," the story of a border plant living on the edge of a garden, and "A Crack in the Sidewalk," about flowers that bring beauty to a big city.

Snapdragons: The Adventure Award goes to the star of the swashbuckling and colorful "Dragons in My Garden," by Low-Water Needs Productions.

Honorable mention in the adventure category is awarded to red salvia, for its brilliant red display in "Call Me Firecracker!"

Congratulations, all!

MAKE A MAY BASKET

Roman children made May baskets to celebrate Floralia, or May Day (May 1) in honor of the goddess, Flora. Today, the fun of a May basket is surprising a neighbor and celebrating May blooms, by leaving the basket at someone's door, ringing the bell, and running away!

To make a May basket, you'll need construction paper, ribbon, and flowers. A paper lace doily on the edge of the basket is nice if you have one.

Roll the paper into a cone. Staple or glue it together. Staple the ribbon to each side of the basket. Edge the top with a paper doily.

Then gather flowers, wrap a wet paper towel around their stems, and wrap the paper towel with a recycled small plastic baggy, attached loosely with a rubber band.

What a great May surprise!

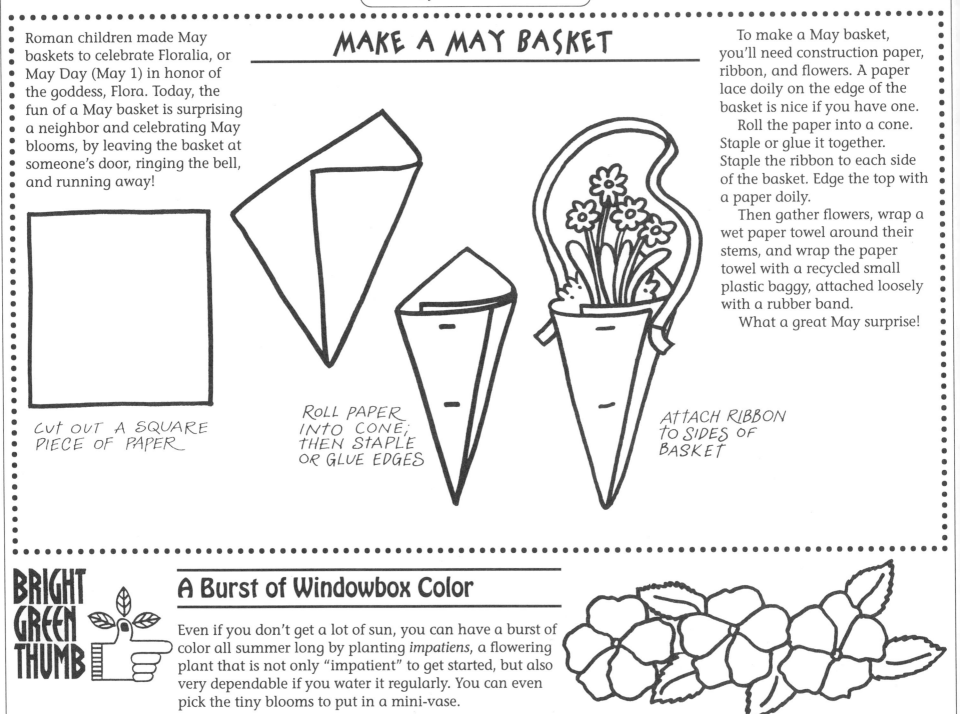

CUT OUT A SQUARE PIECE OF PAPER

ROLL PAPER INTO CONE; THEN STAPLE OR GLUE EDGES

ATTACH RIBBON TO SIDES OF BASKET

BRIGHT GREEN THUMB

A Burst of Windowbox Color

Even if you don't get a lot of sun, you can have a burst of color all summer long by planting *impatiens*, a flowering plant that is not only "impatient" to get started, but also very dependable if you water it regularly. You can even pick the tiny blooms to put in a mini-vase.

SHOW THEM OFF!

You've dug the dirt and planted the seeds, watered, fed, sung to, and loved the flowers growing in your pot, patch, plot, or community garden down the block. Now, the results are blooming!

Make them last: Follow these simple rules to have cut flowers that last and last:

1 Pick flowers in the morning or late afternoon, but not when the sun is hot.

2 Bring an old coffee can filled with water out to the garden with you. Cut the longest stem you can and place in the water immediately.

3 Use sharp scissors to make a smooth, slanted cut. Handle scissors carefully — ask a grown-up to supervise.

A ONE-OF-A-KIND CREATION

When you place flowers in a vase, you are creating a work of art! And like all art, you'll want to think about color, balance, shape, size, and impact.

Hey! Where's a vase?: Look for a container for your flowers that matches their size and color. Let your imagination and artistic expression take flight when it comes to vases. Create a vase from anything that holds water, including painted salad dressing jars, old sugar bowls, and plastic containers tucked in baskets or painted lunch bags!

Shape and color: What shape do you want to create? Would you like your flowers shaped like a fan? Or in a round puff? Or maybe an abstract design? Will it be a solid mass of one color, a burst of many colors, or a single stem of simple beauty?

Balance: Balance is the basic rule of flower arranging. Without it, flowers might tip over or — horrors! — be hidden from view. Put the big, "heavy" flowers in the center. Let the lighter, smaller flowers ride on top and on the sides.

Steady as she goes!: To hold your flowers in place, put some pieces of a hedge or stiff shrub in the bottom of your vase. Or, put a bunch of marbles in the bottom of the vase.

Extra pizzazz: Add some unusual greens such as asparagus ferns, wild grasses, shiny leaves, or evergreen needles to your arrangement.

PLASTIC TUB   PAPER BAG   GLASS JAR

FAN SHAPE

PUFF SHAPE

BALANCE   MARBLE HOLDER

P.S.!

Kids in Japan are taught flower arranging along with reading, writing, and arithmetic. Japanese people know that attractive flower arrangements are good for the mind, heart, and soul.

GROW A SCENTED GARDEN

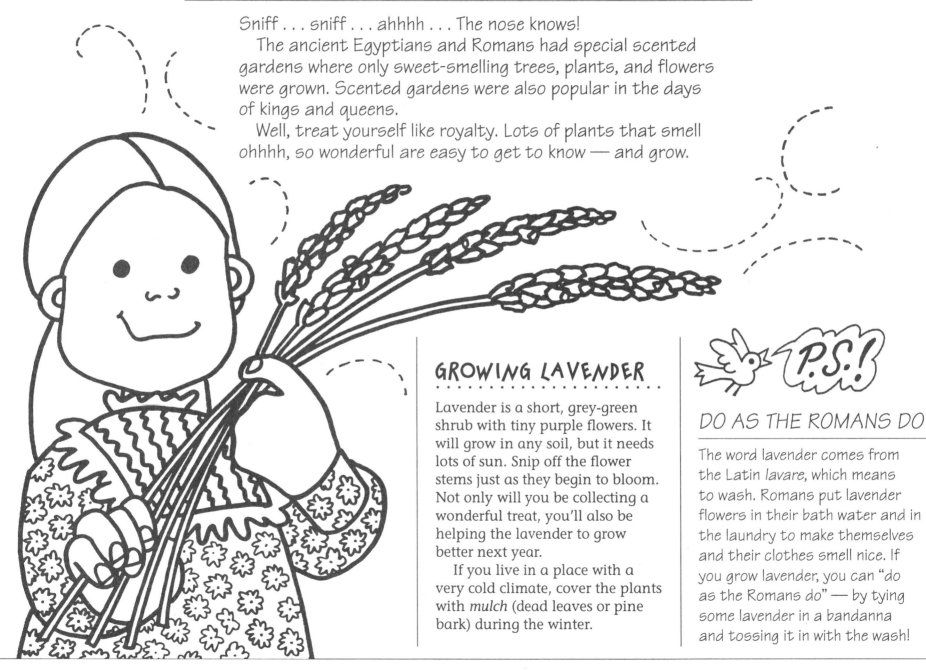

Sniff . . . sniff . . . ahhhh . . . The nose knows!

The ancient Egyptians and Romans had special scented gardens where only sweet-smelling trees, plants, and flowers were grown. Scented gardens were also popular in the days of kings and queens.

Well, treat yourself like royalty. Lots of plants that smell ohhhh, so wonderful are easy to get to know — and grow.

GROWING LAVENDER

Lavender is a short, grey-green shrub with tiny purple flowers. It will grow in any soil, but it needs lots of sun. Snip off the flower stems just as they begin to bloom. Not only will you be collecting a wonderful treat, you'll also be helping the lavender to grow better next year.

If you live in a place with a very cold climate, cover the plants with *mulch* (dead leaves or pine bark) during the winter.

P.S.!

DO AS THE ROMANS DO

The word lavender comes from the Latin *lavare*, which means to wash. Romans put lavender flowers in their bath water and in the laundry to make themselves and their clothes smell nice. If you grow lavender, you can "do as the Romans do" — by tying some lavender in a bandanna and tossing it in with the wash!

Flea-Be-Gone

Guess who hates the smell of lavender? Fleas! If you have a dog or cat, make a collar from lavender to keep pests away (see page 124).

LAVENDER SACHET

Sachet (sa-SHAY) is a bag of sweet-smelling dried flowers that you put in bureau drawers to make everything smell fresh and clean. Lavender flowers make the best sachet in the entire universe!

To make a small (about three inches long) lavender sachet, cut an old handkerchief, or a piece of fine lace or thin cotton into a square or rectangle. Then, bunch lavender flowers in a little bundle, wrap it in the cloth, and tie it with ribbon. Or, you can sew the sachet into a small pillow shape.

CARNATIONS (DIANTHUS)

These graceful perennials are nice to the nose, and if they are happy in your garden, they'll stay for many years.

Rainbow carnations: Would you enjoy a rainbow bouquet? All you need to make it happen are food coloring and white carnations.

Remember your celery stalk experiment (page 23)? Fill six glasses with bright food coloring of red, orange, yellow, green, blue, and purple, and put a white carnation in each glass. After several hours, the flower will begin to take on the color of the water. Give it a day and you'll have a rainbow bouquet!

BLOOMING BULBS!

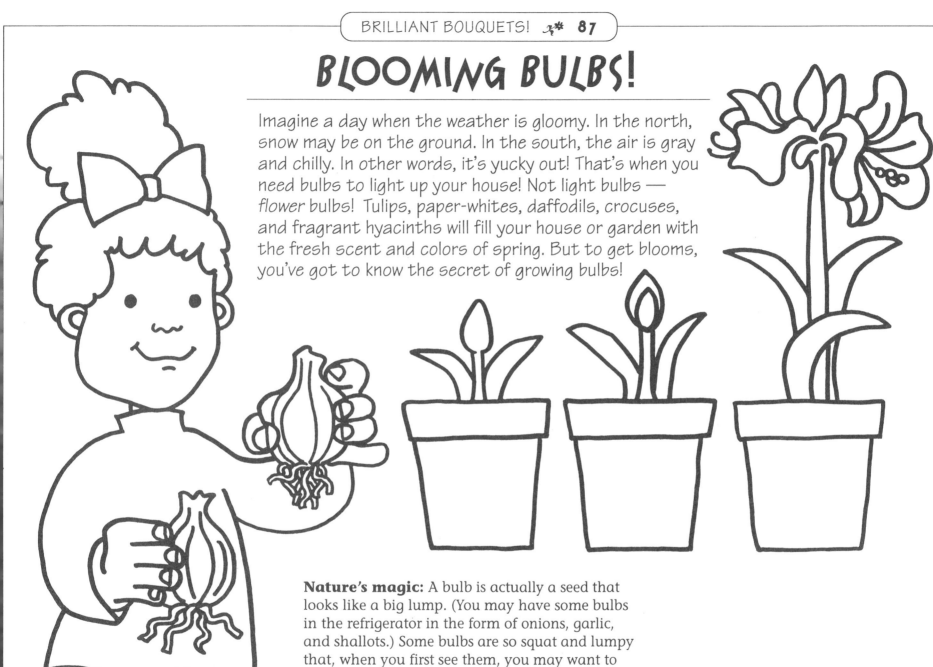

Imagine a day when the weather is gloomy. In the north, snow may be on the ground. In the south, the air is gray and chilly. In other words, it's yucky out! That's when you need bulbs to light up your house! Not light bulbs — *flower bulbs!* Tulips, paper-whites, daffodils, crocuses, and fragrant hyacinths will fill your house or garden with the fresh scent and colors of spring. But to get blooms, you've got to know the secret of growing bulbs!

Nature's magic: A bulb is actually a seed that looks like a big lump. (You may have some bulbs in the refrigerator in the form of onions, garlic, and shallots.) Some bulbs are so squat and lumpy that, when you first see them, you may want to call them *blubs!*

But you'll find out that a flower bulb is the best jack-in-the-box in the world. That lumpy ugly duckling grows into gorgeous, colorful flowers!

FOR OUTIES: SPRINGTIME BLOOMS FROM AUTUMN BULBS

Light up your yard in spring with cheerful daffodils, sweet-smelling hyacinths, and confetti-colored tulips that you plant in the fall, as bulbs. Just follow this old garden rule: *When the first frost spoils your summer garden, get busy planting springtime bulbs!*

PLANTING BULBS

1 Plant the bulbs twice as deep as they are tall.

2 Mix bone meal, a necessary bulb food, in the bottom of the hole before you plant. Scatter a handful on the ground after planting, too.

3 After they've bloomed, the plants will turn yellow and wither. Don't cut them down, though, because they feed the bulb for next year. Gather the withering leaves with a rubber band, or be a leaf stylist and plait them into braids!

DEPENDABLE DAFFODILS

"Daffies" are the world's easiest flowers to grow! Not only that, they will bloom year after year after year!

Some kids like to plant in neat rows. That's fine, but remember to leave space between them (at least two handprints).

Other kids take their bulbs and toss them lightly on the ground, and plant them wherever they fall. That makes for a natural-looking garden in spring.

CROCUS

HYACINTHS

IRIS

ANEMONE

DAFFODIL

TULIP

DAHLIA

FOR INNIES: IT'S BLOOMING ALIVE INSIDE!

When you have pots of purple or pink hyacinths, bright red and yellow tulips, or sparkling white narcissi blooming in your house, you'll see for yourself the flower power inside ordinary-looking bulbs.

Growing bulbs that bloom indoors is called *forcing* the bulbs. We like to think of it more as coaxing them, because the bulbs seem to enjoy producing pretty flowers for pleasure in the great indoors. (For more colorful indoor flowers, see page 112.)

SPRING IN DECEMBER?

You have to be foxy to force bulbs! In nature, bulbs sleep in the cold, winter ground before sending up their beautiful flowers. You'll have to fool your indoor bulbs into believing that winter has come — and gone!

How do you trick a flower bulb? It's easy! You've just got to let it "sleep" in a cold, dark place. Where's the coolest, darkest place in your house? The refrigerator!

A refrigerator is the perfect place for bulbs to snooze: It's cold, but not freezing, and, except when people are looking for snacks, it's nice and dark.

POTTING THE BULBS

Fill the pot halfway with soil and a few tablespoons of bone meal. Then set the bulbs in. They should be close, but not touching one another.

Add the rest of the soil, so that only the tippy-tops of the bulbs stick out. Give the bulbs a good drink of water, and then put the pot in your refrigerator. Sprinkle a little water on them from time to time, but basically, leave them alone.

After eight to ten weeks of refrigeration, move them to a cool, dark place like a closet for another week or two. Water them like a houseplant, whenever their soil gets dry.

When green appears, put the pots in a sunny place — and watch your new plants zoom up and grow! The bulbs think spring has arrived, so they are sending up the stalks that will burst into bloom! What a treat for you and your family on a winter's day!

FILL POT HALFWAY WITH SOIL AND SOME BONE MEAL

SET BULBS, POINTED END UP, ON SOIL, CLOSE BUT NOT TOUCHING

ADD REST OF SOIL WITH TOPS OF BULBS STICKING OUT; THEN WATER AND PUT IN REFRIGERATOR FOR 8 to 10 WEEKS

MOVE POT TO DARK CLOSET, WATER IF DRY; THEN WHEN GREEN SHOOTS APPEAR, PLACE IN A SUNNY SPOT

BRIGHT GREEN THUMB

Plan Ahead!

Ten weeks in the 'fridge and two more in the closet means you need twelve weeks (or about three months) to let your bulbs sleep before they grow and bloom. If you want spring blooms in February, when do you have to plant them?

PERFUME IN A POT: DUTCH HYACINTHS

Forcing Dutch hyacinths will add more than beauty to your house — it will also add perfume! These beautiful flowers send out a strong, sweet scent that can fill a whole room with springtime.

SUPER EASY! PAPER-WHITES AND PEBBLES

Paper-whites are a kind of narcissus that's perfect for forcing. All you need is a shallow bowl filled with pebbles, marble chips, or gravel.

Place the bulbs on the stones and anchor them by putting more pebbles around them. The tops of the bulbs should peek out from the pebbles.

For two or three weeks, keep the bowl in a cool, dark place. Add water every now and then.

After two weeks, bring your paper-whites out where everyone can see them. Soon, they'll be full of lovely, sparkling white blossoms!

BRIGHT GREEN THUMB

More Pebble Bloomers

The pebble method of forcing bulbs works with other kinds of small bulbs, too. Try growing lilies-of-the-valley, or purple, yellow, or white crocuses by this easy method, too. You'll be happy with the blooming results!

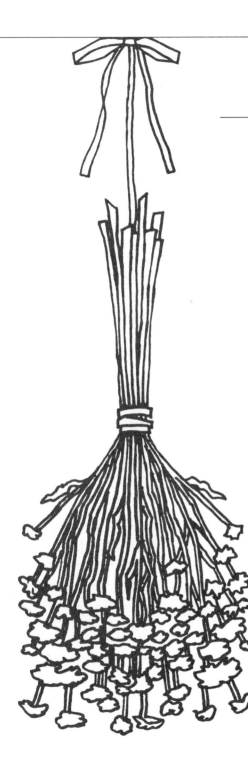

LASTING PLEASURES

DRIED FLOWERS

You can enjoy flowers over and over again — if you dry them! Hang them from a beam on the ceiling, a picture hook, or keep them in a vase.

To dry flowers, be sure to pick them early in the day, then hang them upside down in any dark, airy place, like a garage. For more brightly colored dry flowers, place your flowers in an empty shoe box, trickle sand over them until they are covered, and wait for two to four weeks.

No sand handy? Then make a drying mix of two parts cornmeal to one part borax (available in grocery or health-food stores). No cornmeal or borax handy? Use clean, unscented kitty litter. Really — it works!

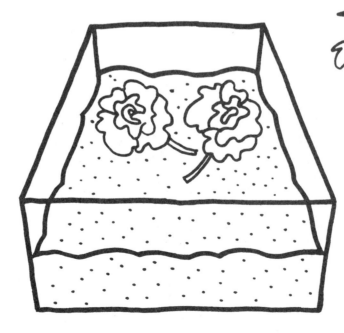

FADED COLOR? GET OUT YOUR PAINTS!

If your pressed flower colors fade, get out your watercolors and paint new color in. Your pressed flowers will look fantastic when they are finished!

CLEVER KID'S FLOWER PRESS

Pressed flowers have been flattened and dried so they can be enjoyed for years. Some people use a fancy flower press, but the truth is, all you need are a few heavy phone books. Lay the flowers down between the pages — leaves, stems, and blossoms — and then close the book on them! Let them sit for two weeks to dry.

MAKE A BOOKMARK

A pressed flower bookmark is a small but thoughtful gift that serves a great purpose. If you like to read, you know what we mean!

To make a bookmark, cover a piece of cardboard with wrapping paper or watercolor paints; then glue a pressed flower on it. Cover with clear contact paper. Punch a hole near the top and tie a 3-inch (8 cm) ribbon in it for easy handling. Add your name and the name of the flower on the back of the marker in ink.

Dear Auntie,
I picked this flower just for you from my garden.

Hello!

PRESSED FLOWER STATIONERY

Cut an oval of construction paper in a color that goes well with your pressed flower. Glue the flower to the paper and glue the paper to a sheet of paper suitable for stationery. You'll be proud to send a letter written on such beautiful, one-of-a-kind paper!

GREEN HOUSEPETS- OOPS! HOUSEPLANTS

They never tip over the litter box. You don't have to walk them. And not one has ever flown away! Houseplants may be quiet, but they sure make good pets!

Think about the pleasure that leafy creatures give — their mysterious way of making people feel good. Maybe it's because they clean the air, or because they're peaceful and calm. Maybe they remind us of nature and the great outdoors.

Either way, when you add a healthy plant to your household, you're making the whole world a little more friendly.

FIVE GOOF-PROOF GREEN HOUSEPETS

You may not realize that indoor air pollution is a problem, but it is — a big one. Bring the green plants to the rescue! Houseplants such as Boston ferns, pot mums, palms, ivy, weeping figs, philodendrons, and the microbes in their soils, are champion air fresheners!

NASA scientists discovered this way to clean up pollution from man-made materials in the spacecraft, Skylab. They pumped toxic air into sealed chambers containing plants, and the results were astounding! Houseplants gobble up pollution like we eat mashed potatoes.

MEET PHIL

Meet Phil (or Philiss). Phil's a friendly green creature who likes to live with people. The plant's formal name is *philodendron* (fill-oh-DEN-dron). But you can call him plain old Phil.

Phils come with big leaves or little ones, speckled leaves or plain ones. Some like to climb all over the place, but others stand like trees in their pots.

Like all plants, Phil needs air, water, good soil, and attention. But Phil isn't picky. If you have a bright spot, then he likes sun. If your room is on the dark side, he enjoys the shade. Phil's just an easy-growing plant that wants a friendly place to live. How about your house?

BRIGHT GREEN THUMB

How To Get More Phils. . . .

You can buy a philodendron in a store; it doesn't cost much. Or, you can ask for a *cutting* from another Phil that lives at your grandfather's house or with the lady next door. (A cutting is a piece of a plant that grows more plants.)

Snip a piece of stem (with leaf) about four inches (10 cm) long and put it in water. Phil will start growing new roots. When they are as long as the tips of your fingers, plant Phil in his own little home. A coffee can, an old teakettle, or a used sneaker will do.

DRACAENA, THE CORN PLANT

Dracaena (dray-SEE-nah) or "Dray," is a big baby, but very easy to care for. Like Phil, she can take light, or tolerate dark. Dracaena can be watered a lot or a little, but she prefers the soil to be moist.

Give Dray appreciation and she will reward you by growing thick leaves that help clean the air in your house. Treat her right, and in a few years, she'll be taller than you!

SNAKE PLANT

Even if you're afraid of snakes — and we hope you are not! — you never have to fear the snake plant, or *sansevieria* (san-sa-VEER-ee-ah). These snakes are not only beautiful, they are useful, too. Their tall, graceful leaves are used to make fishing lines, hats, and mats.

If you're lucky, your snake plant may even grow a creamy white flower. One whiff and you'll be enchanted.

Snake plants have a strong will to live, so they last a long time. They do like lots of company though, so plant a few together in the pot.

IVY

Some people call her *Hedera helix* (HED-er-ruh HEE-liks) but you probably know her as Ivy. Ivy's a dark green plant with starlike leaves that climb and climb wherever she's planted. She grew so much on college buildings that they became known as "the halls of ivy." Ivy may not do your homework for you, but with that collegiate reputation, she can help get you in the mood!

Ivy is also a powerhouse air cleaner, recommended by NASA scientists.

And with all these fine qualities, Ivy is still easy to grow. In bright or low light, she does fine. With moist or dryish soil, she's still okay. (Make more ivy with stem cuttings, the same way you make more philodendrons.)

ANOTHER WAY:
PLACE
CUTTINGS
IN MOIST
ROOT
MIXTURE;
THEN
SEAL IN
PLASTIC
BAG

A Shape for Ivy

If you'd like to have fun with your ivy, grow it into a special shape, called a *topiary* (TOH-pee-air-ee).

You'll need a piece of wire that is soft enough to bend, but stiff enough to keep its shape, like a thin wire hanger. Form the wire into a shape that you like — a heart, star, bird, boat, teddy bear — whatever. Work from the center of the wire, so that you can put the ends into the pot.

Ivy will know what to do next! As the weeks go by, she will climb up and around the wire, until the shape you made is living green!

BOSTON OR DALLAS FERN

You don't have to live in Boston or Dallas to like these ferns. They're lovely to look at, easy to grow, and great air cleaners, too. Put them in good light, but not in direct sun. Ferns were around in the dinosaur age when the climate was hot and moist. Even today, ferns love moist air and soil.

BRIGHT GREEN THUMB

Scrub-a-Dub-Dub

Spritz your houseplants from time to time. Many houseplants — especially large, broadleafed ones — love an occasional real shower, too, to get the dust off and help them breathe more easily.

P.S.!

A HOUSEPLANT ZOO

You can have a personal menagerie by collecting different plants that are named for animals! Here are some easy-to-tame houseplants: snake plant, zebra plant, shrimp plant, rabbit's-foot fern, spider plant, monkey-puzzle plant, flamingo plant, and goldfish plant!

CARING FOR YOUR HOUSEPLANTS

When you care for your green friends you will be rewarded with their beauty and fresh air. But the biggest reward will be the feeling you get when you connect with nature. That's so valuable, it can't be bought in any store!

Caring for houseplants is easy, too, once you understand what they need.

POTTING A PLANT

Potting a plant means making a home for it. Use a suitable pot (see page 102) and put a layer of pebbles or broken pottery on the bottom. Fill the pot halfway up with potting soil. It's easy to make (see page 38) or buy at a supermarket.

Place the plant in and gently spread out the roots with your fingers. Add more soil, and press it down. Water the plant, thank it for cleaning the air, and place it where you will see it often. With that kind of attention, your plant will be off to a good start!

OUCH! IT'S TOO TIGHT!

Just like you, your plant is growing!
You can't wear clothes from last year
— they'd be too tight. Well, the
same goes for your plants. In time,
they may outgrow their pots.

Check your pot's drain hole. If
you see roots poking out, that's like
someone's toes poking out of a too-
tight sneaker. Find a pot one size
larger, and give your plant a bigger
home. This is called *potting up*.

CREATING CONTAINERS FOR YOUR PLANTS

When it comes to making a home for your houseplants, let your imagination fly! Any container that can hold dirt and water, and has a small drainage hole to let water out, can work as a planter. You'll also want an old saucer or dish to keep the pot in and a coaster or flat piece of cork to protect the furniture you place your plant on.

Check around your house for these potential plant homes: Old roller skates, shoes, or sneakers make interesting plant holders, and you can even roll the skates from sunny place to sunny place! Or how about housing a plant in an unused piggy bank, or umbrella stand? Maybe you'll find an old jug, teapot or coffeepot that would look good with a plant living in it. Or use an old sugar bowl, saucepan, dog food dish, cookie jar, vase, or even an empty coconut shell. The choice is yours!

MAKE A PLANT POT

How about raiding the recycling bin to find potential planters? You can plant in the bottom half of a plastic milk jug or an empty food can. All those containers need is a hole for drainage on the bottom (punch hole with a nail), and the chance to hold a plant.

Decorate your containers: A recycled container will need a touch of creativity to jazz it up. One quick way to make a classy-looking container is to put a plain one inside a wicker basket.

No wicker basket? How about decorating a brown paper bag and placing a tin-can planter inside?

A TOUCH OF CLASS

You can make an awesome planter by gluing twine or yarn around a plain old coffee can or plastic peanut butter jar.

YOU'LL NEED:

White glue

3 – 4 yards (2–3 m) of twine, yarn, or thin ribbon

Jar or can

Soak the twine in white glue and slowly wind it around a jar or can that's been smeared with glue. (The glue will dry clear.) Wind from the bottom of the can to the top. You can match the yarn color to your room, or use a natural twine color. Either way, the recycled can will be transformed into a fab "designer" planter!

ART IN THE GARDEN

Clay pots are traditional and inexpensive plant holders that come in many sizes. If you are using a new clay pot, soak it in water for an hour before you plant.

Paint the pot with acrylic paint or tint it with watercolors to give it a sophisticated, artistic look.

FEED ME!

When a plant lives outdoors, it sends its roots deep into the earth to get the food it needs. Your houseplants can't do that, though. They need you to feed them.

Sprinkle them with compost in the spring and in summer. (Wintertime is a kind of rest time for houseplants when they need less water and food.) To make compost indoors, see page 39.

You can also feed them with special plant food, called *fertilizer*. We think the liquid kind is easiest to use. Just add it to their water every two weeks or so.

Don't overfeed your plants though! Plants don't like being overfed any more than people do.

WATER, PLEASE!

Here are three rules about watering houseplants:

1 Use lukewarm water. You wouldn't like cold water dumped on your head, and neither do plants!

2 Put a drip catcher at the bottom of the pot. (Plastic lids are good for this.) Empty the catcher after you water.

3 Mist your plants now and then to keep them clean and refreshed.

MAKE AN AUTO-MATIC WATERER

To make an automatic plant waterer, bury one end of a thick string in the plant soil and the other end in a pail of water. The string will carry the water to the soil automatically!

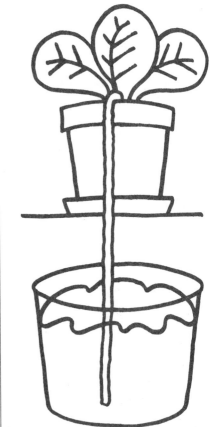

BRIGHT GREEN THUMB

Don't Get Bugged!

If tiny pests start bothering your plants, search and destroy without delay! Be ruthless — the plant you save may be your own! (See page 149.)

LONG-DISTANCE PLANT CARE

When you go on vacation for just a few days, give your plants a good drink before you go. Sometimes it helps to put the plants all together and set them on trays full of moist pebbles. That keeps them moist longer. (See automatic waterer, page 104.)

If you are going away for fewer than three weeks, you can make a miniature greenhouse for the small plants. Cover the large ones with clear plastic (like a dry-cleaning bag), propped up with sticks or wire hangers.

Or place your plants together in the bathtub. Place a sheet of plastic on the bottom and lay wet newspapers on it. Give your plants a good, long drink, then set them on the wet newspapers. Cover the plants with plastic, then go away and enjoy your vacation!

P.S.!

Plant sitting when your neighbors go on vacation is a way to grow cool cash!

PLAYING WITH YOUR PLANT PETS

CREATE A JUNGLE IN YOUR ROOM

Plants like to live in groups, and they like animals, too. If you have more than one plant, you have the beginning of a jungle. For jungle animals, raid your old toy box. We'll bet you have a rubber monkey, plastic tiger, or miniature dinosaur that would look awesome in a jungle display.

Your jungle can live on a table or on the floor. Old action figures can prowl through it, looking for adventure.

WELCOME A BABY WITH A JADE PLANT

If you have a new cousin or know a baby is about to be born, pot a baby jade plant and give it as a gift! A jade plant looks like a small tree with thick, shiny leaves.

This jewel of a plant will grow as the baby does. When the baby is a big kid, he or she will still have the living gift you gave! What a great way to say, "Welcome to the world!"

Holiday Houseplants

When a special holiday or birthday comes, everyone likes to celebrate. Why not your plants? During the winter holidays, you can dress them with tiny holiday balls, made from foil, as mini Christmas trees or Chanukah bushes. Some kids even get permission to string lights around their plants!

For Valentine's Day, tie red ribbons loosely around the stems. On the Fourth of July, stick some miniature flags on them. Grow shamrocks for St. Patrick's Day or sprinkle colored gravel around your plants.

In summer, small paper umbrellas from the local party store look nice on plants, too, especially if you're having a party. Houseplants like a little fun in their lives, too!

HOUSEPLANT VACATION

Houseplants like vacations, just like we do. Mild weather is the perfect time to bring them to the great outdoors to visit their chums who live in nature.

When you first take them out, put your plants in the shade. In a day or two, move the sun-lovers to a sunny place.

You may be surprised to see how big your houseplants grow during their time outdoors. (They may need bigger pots when they come back in! See page 101.)

MAKE A WISH IN A DISH

A finger-sized knight stands under a leafy, green tree made of fern. He holds up a sword, defending his land...

Rubber fish swim in a cement river that divides a field of baby's tears from a moss meadow...

A plastic mermaid basks on the shores of a miniature pond. Across from her, a trumpet flower blooms in bright orange...

A color changer car races down a dirt road, past a fern forest...

You make a piece of world when you create your own dish garden!

WELCOME, ACTION FIGURES

Dish gardens are miniature landscapes, complete with living greenery and figures to populate the place.

YOU'LL NEED:

Deep dish, bowl, or wide flowerpot

Small action figures

Small pebbles

Potting soil

Plants

Of course, the biggest ingredient in any dish garden is your imagination!

Raid your old toy box to find retired action figures, little people and animals, pieces of plastic fences, small buildings, bridges, and vehicles. (Fish-supply stores sell ceramic bridges and other little figures, too.)

Put a layer of pebbles on the bottom of your dish garden container, and fill in the "land" with potting soil.

To landscape, look for baby plants shaped like trees, such as *aralia* (Hercules' club) or miniature palms. *Baby's tears* and *selaginella* are good wish dish "ground" covers.

To add a river or pond: You can even create a river or pond in your dish world.

YOU'LL NEED:

About a half-gallon of dry cement

Old container for mixing

Patience

For a river, sculpt two walls in an S shape from one side of the dish to the other. (Put your hands inside plastic bags to work the cement and keep clean.) Add glass stones or marbles to the river before the cement dries for sparkle in the water.

To make a pond or lake, build up a cylinder shape of wet cement and then press the pond in with your fingers or an old cup. Wait two whole days for the cement to dry; then fill the dish with soil. To water your dish garden just keep the river or pond filled up!

Science Sense

A Rainforest in a Bottle

Have you ever created a *terrarium*? A terrarium is a complete *ecosystem* in a jar — plants, soil, food, light, air, and water. To learn how to make one, look in the library in a nature book or in a book we wrote called, *Kids & Weekends: Creative Ways to Make Special Days*. There, you'll also find how to make a vivarium — a terrarium with small animals, too.

A CACTUS GARDEN

Desert plants like *cacti* and *succulents* (aloe, ice plant, burro's tails) are the camels of the plant world, storing water inside themselves.

The beauty of every desert plant is unique, and a collection of them in one pot is awesome. Unlike most plants, cacti love heat, so in winter, you can even keep this garden on the heater!

1 Look for a wide, shallow container to show off your plants. Cacti do not need deep pots because they have very short roots. Choose an assortment of four to five young plants from a garden center or florist.

2 When you put your garden together, remember to protect your hands with thimbles and gloves. (The tiny prickles on young cacti can really hurt!)

3 Use potting soil that is mixed with sand. Fill the pot halfway up, set in the cacti, and fill in the rest with soil. Leave room for a layer of pure sand, though, to give your cactus garden a real desert look.

4 To add the sand, use a funnel, or a sheet of rolled-up paper. Otherwise, the sand will stick to the tiny thorns on your cacti. (If you ever need to clean the thorns, use a cotton swab.)

5 Water when you first plant, and then only when the soil becomes quite dry. Cacti rot if overwatered. Keep in a sunny room and feed with plant food once a month.

Science Sense

Frankenstein's Cactus

Yes, Dr. Frankenstein, you can invent a one-of-a-kind cactus, by *grafting* the head of one cactus to the body of another! Grafting means joining plants together. When you graft your cacti, you'll be making a plant that nature never thought of — until you came along!

The best time to graft your cacti is from May to October, when desert plants are in their growing season. In just a day or two you will have created a living creature with the body of one plant and the head of another!

YOU'LL NEED:

Sterilized, sharp knife (and a grown-up's permission to use it)

Cutting board

String or rubber bands

2 healthy cacti that fit well together

GIVE YOUR NEW CREATION A NAME

The cactus you make by grafting is a new, never-before-seen creation. Why not give it a new, never-before-heard name?

You can give the new plant a common name and a formal name, too. If your name is Matt, you could call it Mattious inventious, or for short, Mr. M.

Or, how about calling it Brandius newius? Or even Weirdium thingium!

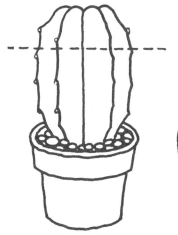
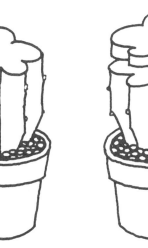

1 Slice off the top of the cactus that will be the bottom plant. To keep the surface moist, cut a thin slice off the piece you just removed and lay it on the surface of the remaining piece where you cut.

2 Slice off the top of the plant that you want to graft. You can use a new shoot of growth or a plump tip as long as the cuts are similar sizes. If there is a lot of sap running, wash it off with water. Keeping the cut clean is very important!

3 Remove the thin, covering slice, if you made one, and join the two plants together, pressing them gently. Attach the parts with string or rubber bands. (You can join the parts with toothpicks, but these will leave a small scar when you remove them.)

4 Put your new creation in a shady place for a day or two. (And please don't try to take the plant apart to see if it has really joined. That would be like digging up seeds to see if they are growing!)

SEVEN SUPER BLOOMERS

Color your world with flowering houseplants! They come in white, red, pink, orange, purple, and yellow. They flower in winter, summer, autumn, or spring. Flowering houseplants are bright and cheerful. Tie a ribbon around its pot and you've got an instant gift, too!

ZEBRA PLANT

With striped leaves that look like a green and white zebra, this plant's bold, sunshiny yellow flowers bloom in autumn.

Your zebra will like moist soil and lots of light, but not hot sun. To keep it blooming year after year, follow these easy rules. When it finishes flowering, cut the plant down to just a couple of leaves. When a side shoot appears, change the plant's soil. You'll have beautiful flowers again next year!

To make more zebra plants, cut off a side shoot and stick it in warm, sandy soil.

CYCLAMEN

Also called the poor man's orchid, the cyclamen (SY-kluh-men) sends up slender stems with pink, lavender, or rose-colored blossoms that cheer up any winter day. Its leaves are a lovely heart-shape.

Like the zebra plant, cyclamen likes light but not direct sun, and a little — not a lot of — water.

Pretty Useful

Sphagnum (SFAG-num) *moss* makes great mulch for houseplants. Mulch is stuff that you put around a plant to keep it weed-free and to give it extra food. Sphagnum moss has friendly chemicals that keep pests away, and it also keeps soil from drying out.

POINSETTIA

The bright red "flower" of this famous Christmas plant is actually not a flower at all — the "petals" are special top leaves of the plant, called *bracts*! If you live in a warm climate, you can plant your poinsettia outside after the holidays and grow it like a shrub. If leaves fall off, you know you have watered it too much.

GARDENIAS

A gardenia will fill your home with sweet blossoms in summer, and grace it the rest of the year with glossy, dark-green leaves. Gardenias like lots of sun and water, especially when they bloom.

GLOXINIA

Grow gloxinia indoors or out. It's got velvety leaves and beautiful flowers. Keep the soil moist but not soggy, and put it in a place with lots of light, but not hot sun. Your gloxinia will reward you with its lovely flowers.

When the flowers are finished and the leaves have withered, dig up the plant and remove the thick stem, or *tuber*. Store the tuber in a cool, dark place, and plant it again next winter for more beautiful blooms.

PAPER FLOWER

The paper flower or *bougain-villea* (boo-gun-VEE-ya), isn't much until it blooms, but oh! what a sight when the flowers come in summer! Then, the plant is a mass of pink or red. Feed it often in spring and summer, and keep it in the same pot all its life. Water when it's flowering and less when it's not.

Make new paper flowers by cutting the stems (as you would with a philodendron).

BRIGHT GREEN THUMB

Add earthworms to the soil of your indoor plants to keep them super healthy! Feed the worms a spoonful of buried kitchen scraps once or twice a week, and watch your plants grow!

AFRICAN VIOLETS

African violets are some of the loveliest, bloomingest plants around. They are so popular that there are special clubs for people who love them.

To bloom, give your African violets lots of sun and bright light all day. (You may need a grow light if you don't have lots of sunshine.)

When you water your African violet, water the soil, not the leaves. Or, put water in the drip catcher and wait for the roots to slurp it up.

Check out special food for your violets at your local greenhouse or gardening supply center. (This special attention is a small price to pay for African violets!)

To start more African violets place the stem of a leaf in water, until it sprouts tiny roots. Then, plant in its own small pot.

When a Plant Dies

Artist in Bloom

Like all living things, plants die. Some die of old age; some die of too much, or too little, water. Some die when there's a frost, and some expire from too much heat.

If you have lost a favorite plant, write a poem about it. Your poem can tell about the way the plant made you feel, and how much you enjoyed it while it was alive.

GOODBYE, IVY

Goodbye, Ivy, you were nice
I watered you once, I watered you twice
Then from the window sill you fell
You broke your leaves, and stem as well
You're gone now, but I'll remember
You as compost next September.

HERBS FOR OOMPH!

They jazz up our salads and perk up our drinks. They soothe our spirits, and rashes, too. They freshen up our closets, and add zest to our soup!

To **botanists**, the people who study plants and their ways, an **herb** (pronounced ERB in America, HERB in England) is a plant that dies back to the ground each winter and has no woody stem. But to most people, an herb is any plant that's useful in the house as a flavoring, tea, or medicine.

Terrific taste is a snip away when you grow herbs. A sprig of mint in your tea or sprinkled in salad, a snip of marjoram tossed in spaghetti sauce, a sprig of parsley served on potatoes — herbs give extra oomph! and super zest to everything!

A LIVING SPICE RACK

A window box is the perfect place for an herb garden. It's a living spice rack filled with fancy flavors!

Window boxes can be made from plastic or wood. Just make sure that yours has a drain hole at the bottom.

A layer of sphagnum moss (see page 112) and a few pebbles on the bottom of the box are useful, too, because they will help the roots of your window-box plants hold water longer.

Herb seeds take several weeks to sprout. To enjoy them in a hurry, you may want to plant seedlings from your local gardening center.

CHIVES

ROSEMARY

BASIL

THYME

PARSLEY

SAGE

INNIES AND OUTIES! GROW AN HERB GARDEN

. . . on your window sill, out on the deck, or on the side of the house. Most herbs do great in pots, so long as their roots have room to grow. *Parsley*, for instance, is as pretty as a picture and terrific to taste. It grows indoors or out, in a pot or in the ground.

If you love parsley, grow two or three plants. You will want to snip off leaves often; that way the plants can take turns giving and having a rest.

Other herbs that taste terrific are *marjoram, oregano, thyme*, and *tarragon*. All grow indoors or out.

NATURE'S MEDICINE CHEST

Back in the Stone Age, people discovered that some plants have amazing healing powers. The first medicines all came from plants.

Plants are still an important source of medicine. Aspirin, for instance, comes from the bark of the willow tree. Native Americans shared the bark with the first settlers, and years later, scientists used the formula to make the "modern" pain reliever. Today, some scientists are returning to nature hoping to discover more useful medicines. They travel the world, making friends with tribal leaders to learn the secrets of healing plants.

AH-CHOO!

Did you sneeze? Quick! Get some *echinacea* (ech-ih-NAY-sha), or purple cone flower. Some say this garden flower takes the power out of a cold! Ask a grown-up to boil the root of the plant in water, then strain and drink.

Many people believe that if you drink echinacea tea, you will never even get a cold in the first place! Well, there's one way to find out for yourself. Bottoms up!

AGGHH! SORE THROAT...

If your throat hurts, try drinking hollyhock tea. Hollyhocks have been used for ages to soothe sore throats and earaches.

Make tea from the flowers, and sip it slowly. Do you feel the fire in your throat going out?

OUCH! A BAD BRUISE!

If you fell off your bike, go get mother — mother-of-thyme, that is. This low-growing herb is not just a tasty spice, some people say it's soothing on scrapes and bruises.

Make the strongest tea that you can, using just 1/4 cup (50 ml) of water. After it cools, pour the liquid on a clean cloth. Put the cloth on your bruise and keep it there as a compress. Add more liquid from "thyme to time."

STRESSED OUT, YOU SAY? SIP SOME BASIL!

Did you trip over the dog food just as your dad was complaining about you skating in the house? Or maybe you lost your math book, or your baby brother just ruined a favorite work of art. Hey, everybody gets stressed out sometimes.

Don't get upset. Get basil. Crush the leaves and make yourself tea. It may not be the kind of tea that goes well with bread and jam, but it may help calm you down and cheer you up.

UGH! TOO MANY SWEETS

When Peter Rabbit got into trouble in Farmer MacGregor's garden, his mother recommended chamomile tea. She was one smart rabbit mother.

Chamomile helps "settle" a stomach that's been abused with too much food. Next time, don't go for that big bag of candy — but if you do, thank goodness for chamomile tea!

BEAUTIFUL HOUSEPLANT, OR NATURE'S FIRST-AID KIT?

The aloe plant is both! Its light green "spikes" have a substance inside that is used all over the world as a face cream, shampoo, sore-throat cure, and especially, as first aid for minor burns.

If you, or someone you know, gets a minor burn, cut off a leaf and squeeze some of the clear gel onto the burn. This living first-aid kit may soothe your skin.

TEATIME!

GROW A CUP OF TEA

Ah, teatime! Time to relax. Time to talk to a friend, or just talk to your soul. With herbs in your garden, you'll have a steady supply of tasty tea without ever leaving home, or paying at the supermarket.

And talk about fresh-brewed! Your tea will have been growing just minutes before it landed in your cup!

Good plants for tea: Mint, chamomile, and lemon balm are three herbs that make great tea. They are easy to grow, inside and out, as long as they get lots of sun. To pick tea, snip off the freshest, most tender tips and young leaves of your "tea herbs" before the sun gets too hot. Rinse the leaves and tear them into small pieces.

A perfect pot of tea: Ask a grown-up to supervise boiling water. Pour the hot water into a teapot with about four table-spoons (50 ml) of loose tea, hollyhock flowers, or other herbs. Let the pot steep, or sit, for five minutes. Pour through a strainer and enjoy!

FOOD FUN Iced Tea

To make iced tea, add the leaves to a smaller amount of boiling water, and let them steep a longer time. The idea is to make the tea as strong as possible. While it's warm, add a bit of honey. Then, pour the tea through a strainer over a tall glass of ice, and enjoy!

CELEBRATE!

A Homegrown Tea Party

Tea parties are tons of fun for you and the guests you invite. You can invite a few real, live friends, or some loveable stuffed ones, to your party. Have your party indoors or out.

One of the secrets of having a terrific tea party is setting the table. A tablecloth is a must, even if it's a pillow case working overtime.

Dress up for the party, if you like. (Frilly dresses for the ladies and eyebrow-pencil mustaches for the gents are fun.) Funny accents never hurt either, as in, "My deah fellow, wooould you care for a spot of tea?" and "I say, dahling, doon't you loook loverly!" Serve tiny cucumber sandwiches on crustless bread. Decorate the sandwich plate with a paper doily and some radish roses (see page 53).

A GREENER WORLD

Wintertime Tea from Your Garden

To preserve herbs for winter tea, pick the plants in the morning, when the oils are high and most flavorful. The best time to harvest the tea is right before the flowers bloom.

Cut the whole branch. Rinse the leaves, and tie the stems at the bottom. Then hang the stems, upside-down, in a shady, dust-free place for a couple of weeks. When the plants are dry, remove the leaves. (Use the leftover stems for kindling if you've got a fireplace.)

Store your tea in a dark glass jar, or a tin that's been cleaned with hot water, dried, and lined with waxed paper.

When winter comes, add the tea to boiling water and let it brew. As you sip, think about your garden and how it bloomed in the summer!

SPLISH! SPLASH! AN HERBAL BATH

Rub-a-dub-dub, relaxing in the tub! If you like baths, try adding herbs to the water. Herbal baths are delightful! And what's really fun is making them to order. Are you in the mood for a woodsy bath made from pine needles? Or is a lavender and rose petal bath more your pleasure today?

MAKE A MITT

You can make a bath mitt filled with herbs from a washcloth.

YOU'LL NEED:

Small washcloth or piece of terry cloth

Needle and thread

Fresh or dried herbs

Fold the washcloth and sew, leaving one end open. Put herbs in the mitt. Insert your hand when washing. When your bath is finished, toss out the herbs (you can put them in the compost), and put the mitt in the laundry.

INSERT YOUR HAND TO USE

CHOOSE YOUR BATH STYLE

Here are other ways to enjoy herbs in your bath. What kind do you feel like taking today?

Long and luxurious:

1 Make a cup of strong "tea" from the plants you are using.

2 While the tea is brewing, take a quick shower to get clean.

3 Fill the tub with warm water, and pour the cooled "tea" into your bath mitt.

4 Get in the bath, rub yourself with the mitt, and reee-lax! Ahhhhhh....

Quick shower method: Make "tea," put the leaves in a bath mitt, and use it in the shower. At the end of your shower, rinse off the tea!

A pine bath: Pine has a wonderful, clean scent that's super in the bath. To make a pine bath, gather fresh green needles of a fragrant pine tree, add sage leaves if you have them, a little clove, or mint. Put the leaves and herbs in a bath mitt. If you don't have a bath mitt handy, put the herbs in a folded washcloth. Mmmh — that's very refreshing!

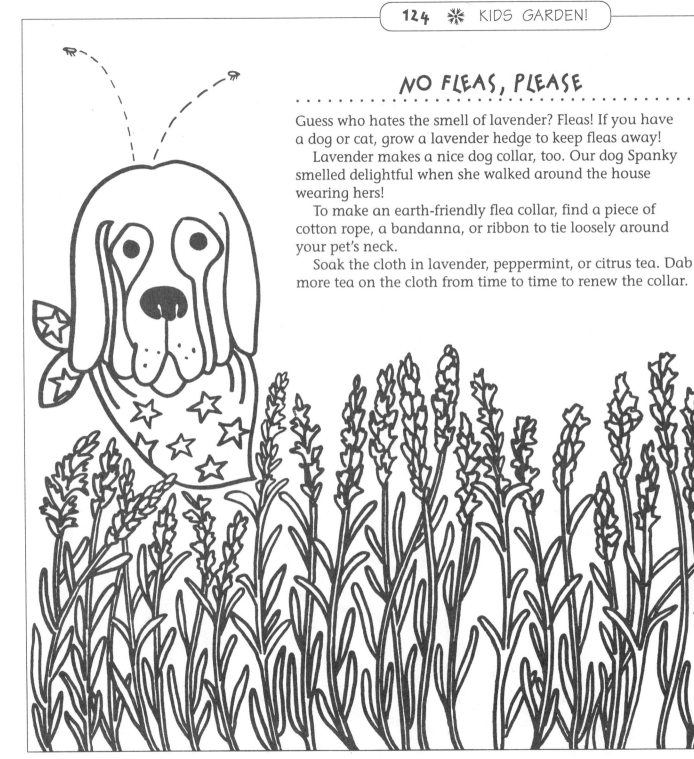

NO FLEAS, PLEASE

Guess who hates the smell of lavender? Fleas! If you have a dog or cat, grow a lavender hedge to keep fleas away!

Lavender makes a nice dog collar, too. Our dog Spanky smelled delightful when she walked around the house wearing hers!

To make an earth-friendly flea collar, find a piece of cotton rope, a bandanna, or ribbon to tie loosely around your pet's neck.

Soak the cloth in lavender, peppermint, or citrus tea. Dab more tea on the cloth from time to time to renew the collar.

A BUTTERFLY CAFE & OTHER SPECIALTY GARDENS

If every person in the world imagined a garden of his or her own, there would be billions of different gardens! That's because each garden is a special, one-of-a-kind creation. What kind of garden will you create?

To spark your imagination, here are some ideas for dream-come-true gardens. Have fun creating!

OPEN A BUTTERFLY CAFE

They are graceful, flying creatures that make us smile! They ride freely, on the wind, fluttering on their fantastic, colorful wings! They are *Lepidoptera* (lep-uh-DAHP-ter-uh) — beautiful butterflies!

Plant a butterfly garden to greatly increase your chances of seeing these fantastic creatures "up close and personal."

BE A GOOD HOST

Butterflies appear in gardens where there are lots of *good hosts*, or plants that butterflies live and feed on. Many of these hosts are wild plants, like milkweed (see page 127), or plants with colorful flowers.

You make your yard a butterfly cafe by serving up plenty of what these brilliant creatures like! On the menu: lantana, lavender, willow trees, zinnias, milkweed, thistle, butterfly bush, butterfly weed, day lilies, phlox, coreopsis (tickseed), and other colorful, sweet-smelling plants.

Science Sense

Is It a Moth or a Butterfly?

You're in the garden enjoying yourself when "it" flutters by, looking oh! so free. Is it a moth or a butterfly?

Hmm... If it's daytime, chances are your flying friend is a butterfly. (Most moths are *nocturnal*, meaning they are more active at night.)

Here's another way to tell the difference between moths and butterflies: Follow your flying friend until it lands. Moths rest with their wings down, but butterflies hold theirs up. While you're looking, check out its antennae. Butterflies have knobs on the ends of theirs; moths' have a feathery look.

BUTTERFLY WEED AND BUTTERFLY BUSH

These plants are so well loved by butterflies that they were named for them! Butterfly weed is a sun-loving perennial (and a relative of milkweed) with bright orange blossoms in summer. Put a marker nearby so you don't forget where it is once the flower fades away for the season. Once the flowers reappear, you'll have lots of butterflies visiting your garden!

Butterfly bush is a *shrub*, or small tree, with long, arching spikes of purple, lilac, red, or white. Each spike has tiny flowers that butterflies love. In late winter, have a grown-up help you prune away last year's growth because flowers only appear on new shoots.

BUTTERFLY WORLD

If you visit Coconut Creek, Florida, stop in at Butterfly World. It's a living museum, full of fluttering butterflies that land on your head and shoulders. It also has beautiful gardens filled with the plants that butterflies love.

WOODSY AND WONDERFUL SHADE GARDENS

If you have a shady place to garden, you'll have to find plants other than zinnias, roses, or tomatoes to grow. You can't fool Mother Nature: When a plant needs sun, it needs sun!

But don't worry. Plants that grow in the shade have a special charm — that of a secret spot in the woods that will almost make you want to whisper.

Your shade garden will be a wonderful place to be even on the hottest summer day!

EIGHT THAT ARE GREAT IN THE SHADE

Bleeding Hearts: Once you plant them, these graceful pink beauties will come back year after year all by themselves! Water them if there's a long dry spell. Bleeding hearts begin their pretty pink show in early spring and keep blooming for over a month.

Begonias: The blooms of this shade-lover are as pretty as a rose. They come in big or small varieties and can be grown from seed. The soil they grow in should be moist, but not wet. At the end of the season, bring them inside, and they'll be happy on a windowsill, waiting for next spring.

Candytuft: Don't eat the candytuft, just let your eyes enjoy the sparkling white flowers. In the fall, dig them up and bring them inside as pretty houseplants!

Daffodils: Not all daffodils are shade-lovers, but if you choose the right kind, they'll do very well in shade (as long as they are not under evergreen trees).

The kind to get are the early-blooming daffies such as "Arctic Gold," "Spellbinder," and "Content." But stay away from the popular "King Alfred" — he's a sun-lover!

Primroses: Gardeners in old England used to plant these pretty springtime flowers along walkways, which led to the expression, "primrose path."

Some people claim that primrose oil is a kind of cure-all, too. One thing is for sure, looking at primroses has to be good for anyone's health!

Violets: "Roses are red and violets are blue" — and so easy to grow that some people treat them like a weed! But not you, because violets make great little bouquets for a May Day basket (see page 82). You can even eat them as salad or snack food. Their leaves and flowers are full of vitamins.

Best of all, the more you pick them, the more they bloom.

Candied Violets

FOOD FUN

In the Court of King Louis of France, candied violets were decorations on the royal cakes! To make this flowery treat, dip violets in beaten egg-white powder, and then in sugar. Let the flowers dry to a sugary crystal. Bon appetit, your highness!

Impatiens: Bright orange! Shocking pink! Spicy salmon! Fire-engine red! Who says you can't grow colorful flowers in the shade?

Impatiens make tons of little flowers! Leave at least 8 inches (20 cm) between them, though, because they spread as they grow. All they need is a little attention and lots of water to bloom, bloom, bloom!

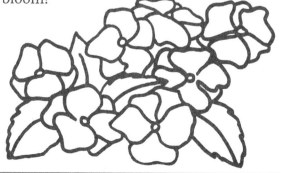

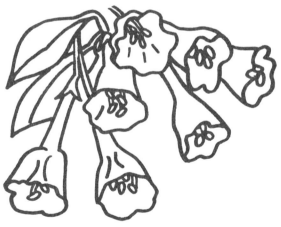

Virginia Bluebells: These pretty bluebells will ring in spring year after year if you plant them in a shady place. They are nature's color changers, too. They start out pink and gradually turn to blue!

BEAUTIFUL LEAVES

In your shade garden, you can also grow plants with such beautiful leaves you won't even notice that they don't have showy flowers!

Fabulous ferns: With their graceful, feathery leaves called *fronds*, ferns are great-looking and easy to care for. The Christmas fern got its name from the ends of its fronds that look like miniature Santa boots! *Common polypody* is another easy-to-care-for, great-looking fern that grows right out of rocks. That's why some people call it "rock cap."

If you are looking for more ferns, try *maidenhair fern.* Like a ballerina, it's dainty-looking, but as strong and hardy as a plant can be!

Colorful coleus: This shade-loving plant has colorful leaves that make it special, indoors or out. Pinch off the flowers to make the plant bushy. When cold weather comes, bring it inside as a colorful houseplant.

Hosta: Plant it once and it will grow forever, with no care at all! Its flowers are slender and graceful, and they smell nice, too. Hosta does a disappearing act in the fall when the weather gets nippy. You'll wonder where it went! But next spring it will burst into bloom again, as bushy and full as ever!

WATER GARDENS FOR INNIES

Do you love to swim? So do some plants! They spend their whole lives floating. Nature designed them to survive in lakes, ponds, swamps, bogs, rivers, streams — and in your room, in a large jar or aquarium!

An underwater garden is an awesome creation, with or without fish in it! Underwater plants come in different shapes and shades of green, yellow, or red. And just think, this is one garden that will never need watering!

A garden for your fish: Fish love plants, just like people do. Underwater plants give fish a place to hide, and keep the water clean. Some species, like angelfish, will only lay eggs on the leaves of a plant. Your pet fish will be very happy to have some plant friends, too!

SETTING UP YOUR GARDEN

All you need for an underwater garden are water, plants, and a place where they can get together. An aquarium is perfect, but so is a large jar.

You can create a work of art by placing your underwater plants in different colors of gravel. The gravel will anchor the roots of the plants to the bottom of the tank. If your underwater garden is in a tall jar, layer different colors of gravel on the bottom to give your garden spectacular stripes. Special rocks and shells add to the world of a water garden, too, as do any waterproof figures you may have around the house.

Buy your water plants in a fish supply store. If you have room, grow a few. Looking at different shades of color and shapes of leaves makes the garden more interesting.

A NEW HUE

If there are no fish in your garden, add a tiny droplet of food coloring to give the water a colorful sheen.

WATER-LOVING PLANTS

Here is a list of water plants that are easy to grow and beautiful to look at:

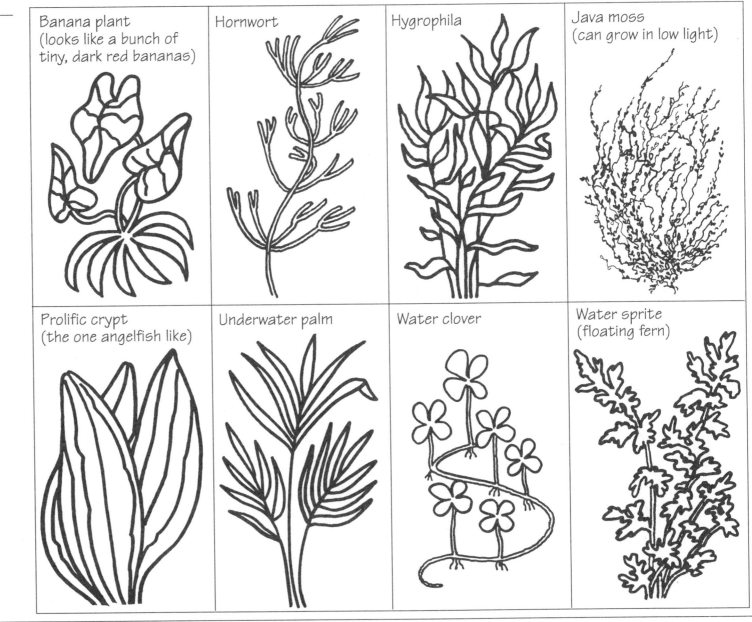

Banana plant (looks like a bunch of tiny, dark red bananas)

Hornwort

Hygrophila

Java moss (can grow in low light)

Prolific crypt (the one angelfish like)

Underwater palm

Water clover

Water sprite (floating fern)

AN OUTIE'S WATERY GARDEN

A COOL POOL IN YOUR GARDEN

If you like flowers, frogs, and the cool feel of water, create a garden pool in your yard or on the deck. Outdoor water plants may look exotic, but they are surprisingly easy to grow.

YOU'LL NEED:

Waterproof container that's at least 12 inches (30 cm) deep

Water plants (see page 131)

Fill your outdoor container or "pool" halfway up with loam (see page 39) in the late spring. Then plant your water plants and fill the pool with clean water.

If you add a fish or two to the pool, ask your pet store owner to recommend a "meat eater" that will nibble up mosquito eggs.

Refresh the water in your pool every few days by bailing out some and adding fresh water. Use the bailed water for your land plants.

12"

On the Deck

If your pool is on a deck, set potted plants around it to give it a great natural look and call it "Hidden Pond." See who notices it first!

In the Yard

If you have a yard, you can bury your pool by digging a hole for it. Put stones around the sides to make it look like a miniature lake.

Then watch for wildlife! The local birds will be happy to have a new source of drinking water and a place to take a bath on a hot day. Don't be surprised if a frog or a water turtle shows up, either! These creatures are attracted to water. Treat them with respect and let them go on their way when they are finished visiting your water garden.

A COLLECTION OF EXOTICS

Do you like strange and unusual things? Does the idea of aliens interest you? Do out-of-the-way places and unheard-of experiences fire your imagination?

Mother Nature is very fascinating. She has created plants that eat meat, and flowers that bloom at night! She's made plants that open and close at the touch of your finger. If you like strange and unusual things, try growing some exotic plants!

Yummy!

BEWARE of PLANT

VENUS'S-FLYTRAP

The Venus's-flytrap is a pleasant little plant — unless you are a meaty insect! The flytrap gobbles up unsuspecting flies and bugs that happen to land on its oblong leaves. Once a creature lands, the leaf closes like a jaw, trapping the victim inside!

If you buy a Venus's-flytrap, feed it bugs and flies. You can even touch the leaf with your finger to get an idea of how the plant holds onto its prey. (Fortunately, you are a big giant who cannot be hurt by its vise-like grip.)

This plant is a natural for terrariums, because it likes lots of moisture in the air. A fishbowl covered with clear plastic (cut from a dry-cleaning bag) makes a good home for this snappy plant, too.

EXOTIC NIGHT BLOOMERS

Some plants, such as moonflowers and night phlox, save their glory for the night.

Moonflowers: Picture big, blooming vines with creamy white flowers and a fragrance that sends you straight to heaven! Like their cousins, morning glories, moonflowers are fast growers that climb anything they can grab hold of. When the sun goes down, the moonflower spreads out, sending a lovely scent into the air.

The secret of growing moonflowers is planting the seed directly into the soil where you want the vine to grow. For some reason that only moonflowers and morning glories know, these flowers refuse to be transplanted — even if you start them in a peat pot.

Oh, well. We all have our likes and dislikes, and flowers are no different.

Zalu, the night phlox: Talk about an exotic name! Try this one on your tongue, *Zaluzianska capensis.* Around our house, we call it, "Zalu." Zalu is a kind of phlox that blooms when the sun goes down. Plant Zalu like ordinary phlox, in rich loam. Be prepared to have your head spin in the most wonderful way when you sniff Zalu blossoms at night — they are pure perfume!

MIMOSA PUDICA

This plant is shy — so shy that it shudders and closes up if you touch it, no matter how lightly! If you're an Outie living in a warm climate, grow it as a tree that bears feathery pink flowers with a sweet, lovely scent. Innies can grow it as a houseplant.

Mimosa likes lots of water and light, and may even produce fluffy flowers in the winter — if it's very comfortable, that is.

OBEDIENCE PLANT

Here's a garden flower, also called false dragon-head, that will not only please you by making lovely flowers, it will also "obey" your touch!

How can that be?

For some strange reason, this plant will keep its stems wherever you place them. If you move the stem so that you can get a better look at a plant in the back of the garden, for example, the obedience plant will stay put — just where it thinks you want it to be!

Maybe you can give one to your favorite teacher as a funny gift!

GROW A BROOM

If you've got a sunny spot in your garden and room for a tall plant, grow yourself a broom! You'll need to get some *broomcorn* seeds at your local garden center, or order them by catalog.

Broomcorn is not really corn; it's a grain called *sorghum*. Sorghum comes from Africa, where it's been used to make brooms for ages. Africans eat the seeds or grind them into flour. Then they use the tufts to make the best brooms in the world.

BROOMS FOR THE BIRDS

Plant the seeds early, because broomcorn plants take about 110 days to develop the straw they're famous for. Your broom will be made from the flowering tops of the plants.

By the way, the birds who visit your yard will be happy that you decided to grow a broom. They love to munch on broomcorn seeds!

MAKING THE BROOM

When your broomcorn plant develops tall tufts, full of flowers or seeds, it's ready to harvest. Cut the plants at the bottom, and hang them upside down in a dry, airy place. After a few days, you can begin *threshing* the tufts to get rid of the seeds.

Threshing is fun. You hold the blunt end of the broomcorn plant and smack it against the ground, or against a handy tree, over and over. Thresh over an old blanket so you can save the seeds for the birds.

When the seeds are off, you're ready to make your broom. If the stems of your plant are strong and stiff, you can wind twine around them tightly, and your broom will be done in a jiffy. Most people need to tie the tufts to a wooden broomstick, such as a straight branch from a hardwood tree.

Your country-styled broom will last a long time!

A ROCK GARDEN

Rocky land may be hard to farm, but it's the best place for a rock garden. If you live on a hill, a rock garden will help to keep your land together, too. Soil that's got rocks on it won't float away when rain comes!

START WITH A ROCK PILE

Find, or dig up, the rocks that will form the "bones" of your garden. Then place them where you want the garden to be. Put the biggest rocks on the bottom and the small ones on top. Every time you make a layer, toss in plenty of good garden soil and press it down with your hands (see page 36). Let some of the rocks show, though. They are too nice-looking to hide.

PLANTING YOUR ROCK GARDEN

Rock gardens need low-growing plants. Plant them so they can creep over the rocks or peek out from a crevice in a rock. That's what is so great about rock gardens — small creeping flowers show up where you least expect them.

Try these if your garden gets sun: sweet alyssum, portulaca, thyme, lavender, and pygmy marigolds.

A shady rock garden can have lily-of-the-valley, primroses, forget-me-nots, and baby ferns.

Any rock garden can have crocuses and daffodils in it, too. They'll give you a head start in spring.

GARDEN IN A SIDEWALK CRACK

City gardeners have to use every scrap of land they can find for their gardens — even a crack in the sidewalk!

To garden in a crack, you'll need to follow all the basic rules of gardening, like preparing the soil so that it's loose and crumbly, with living food like compost or manure.

Then you'll need the right plants. For a flowering sidewalk crack, we recommend sweet alyssum (see page 81). It makes loads of little flowers, and if you live in a warm climate, it will even come back next year.

You may want to plant mother-of-thyme in your sidewalk crack, too. That way, if you want to spice up your salad, you can snip a bit off to toss in! Mother-of-thyme is a hardy plant that can take some foot traffic.

What lucky neighbors you have!

Window-Box Gardens

Petunias, impatiens, periwinkle, marigolds, nasturtiums, and short snapdragons can all thrive in a sunny window-box garden! And if it's food you like to grow, try adding lettuce or parsley plants.

Make your window box the same way you'd make a container for a houseplant (see page 102). You can lighten the soil with vermiculite, or even with some old chopped-up styrofoam cups. That's recycling at its best!

CREATE A WILD SPOT

If you have a yard, one of the best things you can do for nature is to keep part of your property wild. Even if the spot is small, the wild plants that grow in it will feed birds and give shelter to friendly and necessary wildlife. Ladybugs, for example, like to start their lives living on thistle plants, which some people pull as weeds.

A wild spot honors Mother Nature by trusting that she can take care of business.

CARING FOR YOUR WILD SPOT

This is the number one easiest job in the whole world of gardening: Just leave your wild spot alone! Nature will do all the gardening work for you!

Your wild spot will change with the seasons, as plants are born, bloom, and die. It may look a little ragged now and then, but that's okay. You may discover that you like its rugged beauty.

If you live with grown-ups who don't understand the need for a wild spot, and don't want to give you space for one, explain that wild places are an important part of nature. If they still don't approve, ask for a spot behind a bush or in a hidden corner. You can offer to plant a few berry bushes in front of it, to hide it from view.

Giving nature a place of its own, to do whatever it wants to do, is not only generous — it's important.

A WILD POT

Which plots grow wild where you live? You can find out by preparing wild-plant pots. Prepare a pot just as you would for a houseplant (see page 100). Fill it half-way up with potting soil. Then go outdoors and dig up garden soil from the wildest place you know. It can be dirt from the local woods or from behind an old barn. Fill the wild pots with the "wild dirt," water them, and put them in a sunny spot. Keep the soil moist (but not soggy) for a few weeks.

Soon you'll see tiny little plants poking out of the dirt. That's because the soil you find outdoors almost always has seeds of wild plants already in it. What will spring up in your wild pots? You have to grow it to know it!

Make a Marker for Your Wild Spot

Your wild spot or pot will be an interesting attraction in your garden if you put up a sign letting people know what it is.

Try to create a natural-looking marker. Maybe a grown-up will help you whittle some letters out of a chunk of wood. Waterproof paint on a wooden paint stirrer makes a good marker, too.

If you live in a rocky place, put stones around the spot to separate it from the rest of your garden. If you have enough stones, use them to spell out "wild spot."

A SOILLESS GARDEN

Scientists have experimented and found ways to actually grow plants without soil! This kind of gardening is called *hydroponics*, from the Greek words, *hydro*, or water, and *pono*, meaning work. Hydroponic gardening is very important in countries where there is a vast desert, such as Israel and Saudi Arabia. There, people count on hydroponics to produce enough food for them to eat.

Science Sense

Down on the Old Hydroponic Farm

Why don't you plan a nighttime feeding for hydroponic plants? If you said because it is dark outside, you are absolutely right. Even hydroponic plants need light to perform photosynthesis (see page 6).

How well does soilless gardening work? The man who invented hydroponics, Dr. William Gericke, had to pick the first hydroponically grown tomatoes from a ladder! His tomato plants grew over 25 feet (7.5 m) high!

Want to experiment with hydroponics? Try this:

YOU'LL NEED:

Bucket with 5 or 6 holes in the bottom

Large drip catcher (like another large bucket with no holes, or a large cat litter box)

Bag of clean gravel or vermiculite

Hydroponic plant food (sold as "soluble fertilizer" in most garden centers)

Tomato, pepper, or bean seedlings that are at least 6 inches (15 cm) tall

1 Carefully remove each seedling from the soil and shake the dirt off its roots, sprinkling with water to remove any remaining soil. Form a hole in the gravel or vermiculite and place the plant in it.

2 Put the plants in a place where they will get good sunlight.

Twice a day, you will need to "flood" your plants with nutrients. Early morning and mid- to late afternoon are good times. When you feed your plants, let the solution run through their roots, and then "catch" it for the next feeding. Add some (about 10 percent) fresh solution with every feeding, though.

HAIL! HAIL! THE GANG'S ALL HERE!

School gardens, where kids work together to grow things, and *community gardens,* where individuals and families have a small patch of land to grow plants in, are exciting places. See if you can join one!

A community garden gives city people a taste of country life. Community gardeners step through the garden gate into the peaceful but exciting world of nature. To find a community garden in your town, call your local government or The American Community Gardening Association (see page 6).

A school garden gets kids out of the classroom to plant, water, weed, and pick. That sure beats gazing out the window on a beautiful spring day! If your school doesn't have a garden, why not start one?

THE RIGHT STUFF

To create a school garden, you'll need: *enthusiasm, leadership,* and *persistence.*

The enthusiasm will fuel your dream of gardening at school. It takes leadership to get a good team together. And persistence will keep you all going when nothing seems to be going right!

Start by getting your friends excited about having a garden. Come up with a plan and then approach the teachers at your school. The National Gardening Association has a guide to kids' gardening that's chockful of great ideas for school gardens. To order it, or enter one of their contests, write them at 180 Flynn Avenue, Burlington, VT 05401. Good luck, gardeners!

TROUBLE IN PARADISE

They'll arrive on wing. They'll arrive on foot. They'll arrive with their bellies crawling on the ground. No matter how they get there, you can expect plenty of bugs to show up in your garden.

Bugs and insects can help your garden or hurt it. And how you deal with them has a lot to do with how they deal with you!

COMING SOON TO A GARDEN NEAR YOU!

Trouble in the garden usually comes in the form of plant-eating bugs. Some folks swat, squish, or squash any insect that crosses their path!

That's too bad, because most bugs and insects are helpful to human beings and the plants we grow. And insects belong on Earth as much as we do!

Still, we can't have them chomping our tomato plants. So what do we do?

"BAD" [DESTRUCTIVE] VS. "GOOD" [USEFUL]

Bugs that eat our crops aren't doing it to be "bad," of course; they're just trying to survive, like everybody else! Their choice of food is what got them their bad name.

Other bugs, the kind that eat the "bad" ones, are thought of as "good." Get it? This kind of bad-good thinking doesn't reflect the whole truth, of course — that bugs and insects are a part of nature and have the right to be here.

HOW TO GET RID OF DESTRUCTIVE BUGS

The absolute best way to deal with destructive bugs is not to have them in the first place! That means doing what it takes to prevent their coming around. Here are some time-honored ways to keep these bugs away:

1 Plant herbs and flowers that pests hate.

Lavender, rue, chives, mint, and marigolds help keep destructive bugs out.

2 Spread wood ashes around your plants; collar any cutworms.

Fireplace ashes discourage cutworms, flea beetles, slugs, and snails from entering your garden.

Cardboard collars made from a paper cup with the bottom cut off and a slit up the side are good protection against night-feeding cutworms that like to nibble plant stems. Insert the paper or cardboard in the soil around the plant or seedling.

3 Invite birds, bees, toads, and frogs into your garden.

The right creatures are the best pest sheriffs you can find. You may not think that white flies and mites taste good, but to the right bird, they are a delicacy! A frog or toad will love a lunch of fresh cutworms! And be tolerant of your neighborhood skunk for it also eats tons of "bad" bugs.

Chickadees, nuthatches, woodpeckers, and purple martins are birds famous for their bug-eating appetites. Putting up a birdhouse, feeder, and birdbath will give them a royal welcome.

4 The best defense is a good offense.

The minute you spy the first tiny intruders, get out the hose. A blast of cold water goes a long way toward keeping the bug population down! If you can stand it, pick big bugs, snails, and slugs off with your hands.

5 Keep your garden clean.

Cut trouble off at the pass by removing dead leaves and garden clutter where troublesome pests often live. Dead leaves belong in the compost, not the garden.

FRIENDS AND HEROES OF THE BUG WORLD

Here are bugs to encourage in your garden. They eat the ones we want to get rid of. When you see these creatures buzzing or creeping around, put out your arms and say, "Welcome, friend!"

Dragonflies: They don't bite people, but they do munch mosquitos. So let these dragons fly in and do their stuff!

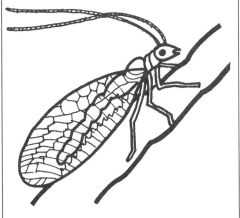

Lacewings are so good at getting rid of pests that you can order them from supply shops. They start life as gray-green worms, but they turn into graceful fliers.

Ladybugs (ladybirds):"Ladybug, ladybug, fly away home!" Let's hope that home is your garden! Because these cute little polka-dotted beetles are good friends in the garden, munching on aphids, scale, mites, and other garden pests.

The larvae of ladybugs are funny-looking, oblong-shaped, orange and black creatures that look like they are growing a toothbrush on their backs. But oh, what good appetites they have! They eat more pests than grown-up ladybugs!

Keeping a wild spot (see page 139) encourages ladybugs, too. They like to nest in thistles and other out-of-the-way "weeds." They go to your garden for lunch and dinner the way you go to a restaurant!

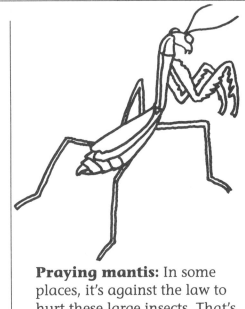

Praying mantis: In some places, it's against the law to hurt these large insects. That's only fair, because praying mantises have saved tons of crops by eating garden pests.

Trichogramma wasps: They're small, but speedy, and best of all, they won't sting you! We call these super little wasps "Trickies" and we're happy to have them in our garden.

BEES, PLEASE

No bees, no flowers. Why? Because bees pollinate flowers.

No bees, no fruit. These fuzzy fliers pollinate fruit trees, too.

No bees, no honey, either. Bees are the ones who created the sweet stuff in the first place!

No bees, no bee stings. Wait a minute! Before you try to swat a bee, try a little bee psychology so you can "live and let live."

BEE PSYCHOLOGY

Are you afraid of bees? Many people are, because bee stings hurt! But here's something to remember. Bees die after they use their stinger. So no self-respecting bee is going to give up its life just to be nasty. *Bees only sting when they think they are going to be killed.*

And nothing makes a bee think it's about to be killed more than a human waving his or her arms and hopping all over the place!

If you see a bee, scream if you want — bees are deaf. But stay as still as possible! The bee will go away as soon as it decides it's not in danger.

To avoid attention from bees in the first place, wear light-colored clothing, and keep your hands free of sugar. Bees are most threatened by rough-textured, dark, moving things that remind them of their worst enemies, bears!

IN A CLASS BY THEMSELVES . . . ANTS!

There are far more of them per pound than there are of us, making them one of the world's dominant creatures. King Solomon and Benjamin Franklin openly admired them. They have been the stars of many stories, ever since people first began telling them.

They are ants — the famous, hard-working creatures who wander our gardens and always will.

Should you discourage ants in the garden?: The answer is yes and no. The trouble with ants is that they keep aphids the way we keep cows! They milk them for the sweet fluid inside them — fluid that was robbed from your garden! Therefore, you should discourage ants in the garden.

But the answer is no, too. For starters, getting rid of ants altogether is impossible. Also, ants do a lot of good, by cleaning up dead bugs and such.

To discourage ants, sweep over any anthills you see too close to your garden. Don't worry about the ants when you do this. They always have a few escape routes and other methods to get in and out.

These little guys are survivors!

BRIGHT GREEN THUMB

Coffee grounds discourage ants from coming around.

TROUBLE IN THE GREAT INDOORS

Just because you're gardening indoors, or in a window box, doesn't mean you're immune to the invasion of troublemakers. Far from it! But there's still a lot you can do, even if you don't have the bees, birds, and ladybugs to help you!

MUGSY BUGSY: AWFUL BUGS, AND HOW TO WIPE THEM OUT!

Mealybugs, aphids, white flies, and spider mites: For houseplants, those are the "baddest" bugs around. These little creatures will eat plants up if you don't watch out!

If you have a magnifying glass, use it for your search-and-destroy mission. Plant pests are tiny, but the damage they do is great! So get ready to take aim and knock them out of the picture and off your plants!

WANTED: THE MEALYBUG GANG

These grayish-white criminals will suck the juices out of your plants before you can say "Scram!" Male mealys resemble tiny white flies; females look like tufts of cotton sitting on the stems of the victim plant — an innocent disguise, but don't let it fool you.

If you spot these deadly creatures, get your weapons ready. You'll need a cotton swab and a sprayer full of soapy water. First, swab the sticky little critters right off the plant. Check under every leaf and around the roots. Take out an inch of soil and replace it, too.

In the garden, blast with a hose. In the house, go to the bathtub, cover the soil with foil, and start blasting with your sprayer! Very soapy water works well against mealys. (Diluted Dr. Bronner's Peppermint Oil Soap, which is sold in health food stores, is perfect.)

One mealy can lay six hundred eggs, so have no mercy! Spray and swab until every bit of white fuzz has been destroyed.

Ta-ta, mealys, hope you have a nice trip — down the drain!

WANTED: APHIDS, AKA PLANT LICE

One aphid can produce almost six billion eggs in a single summer! If you placed them end to end, they would stretch for 112,000 miles! Fortunately, however, aphids have lots of natural predators, like birds, lacewings, ladybugs, and YOU!

Aphids hurt plants the same way mealybugs do, by sucking out their juices. Shades of Dracula!

If you have aphids, spray them with soapy water, as described above. If that doesn't work, don't worry. The plant police, meaning you, have other ways of getting rid of these destructive critters — like the dreaded garlic bath!

Yes, you can get rid of these mini-vampires the same way you'd get rid of Dracula. He wouldn't like sitting in a bath of mashed-up garlic, and neither will they!

WANTED: SPIDER MITE VILLAINS

You can't see them — you just see the damage they do. A bitten leaf here, a nibbled leaf there. Turn over the leaf and inspect with a magnifying glass. If you see a teeny speck of dark brown, or a miniature spider web, you're looking at a deadly killer: the spider mite.

Give the villain the cotton swab send-off, followed by a good splash of soapy water. A dose of garlic bath will hurt him, too!

A BETTER WAY TO PEST CONTROL

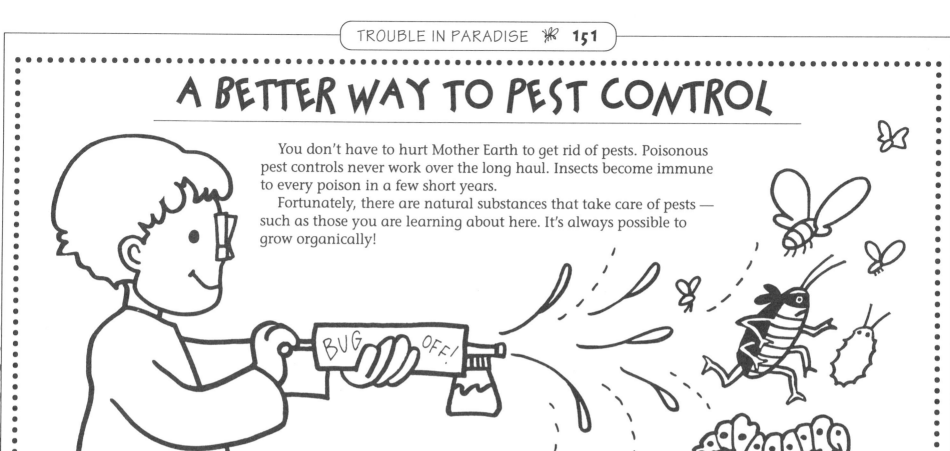

You don't have to hurt Mother Earth to get rid of pests. Poisonous pest controls never work over the long haul. Insects become immune to every poison in a few short years.

Fortunately, there are natural substances that take care of pests — such as those you are learning about here. It's always possible to grow organically!

BATHING IN GARLIC!

To make a garlic bath, mash several cloves of garlic and soak them in water overnight. Add onions and hot pepper, if you want to. By morning, that water will smell garlicky enough to knock a hippo flat on its back. That's just the way you want it.

Strain out the garlic, fill your sprayer with the water, and go to town, blasting your plants. Aphids and other houseplant criminals will swoon right in front of your eyes!

While you've got your sprayer out, you might as well give all your plants a spritz. Garlic spray is not only a cure, it's a good preventive, too. Dousing your plants in garlic water is like hanging up a sign that says, "No bugs allowed."

A POTENT RECIPE FOR PLANT PESTS

Here's another recipe for getting rid of unwanted pests. It's a little more powerful than the soapy water and garlic water treatments, so use it as a last resort.

We call it the DO Die Treatment. The D stands for dishwashing detergent, and the O stands for oil.

Mix 3 tablespoons of dishwashing detergent with 1/3 cup of vegetable oil. The slippery goo you create is a concentrated version of DO Die. Put a couple of spoonfuls into your sprayer, add water, and shake. Then let the creepy pests have it!

WEEDS: WILY INVADERS?

Once, when everything was wild (even people), every plant was a weed. That is, every plant grew where it grew, all by itself.

When people planted the first crude gardens, they realized that in order to grow the plants they wanted, they'd have to discard any competitors! That's how the idea of "weeds" came to be.

When you garden, you, too, will have to get rid of any unwanted plants that may compete for space, soil, and water in your garden. Weeding is a necessary part of gardening.

BRIGHT GREEN THUMB

The secret of easy weeding is to weed when the soil is moist and the weeds are young.

WEED COMPOST

NATURE'S GARDEN GIFTS

We said it before, but we've got to say it again: The best gift you get from your garden is *wisdom*. Here are some of the reasons and ways we think that gardening makes you wise.

1

Gardening is real — it's "all the way" live!

2

When you garden, you discover that life is a process, and that good things are worth the wait.

3

Gardening connects you to Nature, giving you a chance to know it, up close and personal.

4

Gardening is good for the earth. If everybody took care of the land that they were on, the whole earth would become a beautiful garden!

5

A garden feeds our bodies and our souls. It makes our muscles strong and our hearts full.

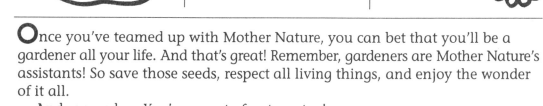

Once you've teamed up with Mother Nature, you can bet that you'll be a gardener all your life. And that's great! Remember, gardeners are Mother Nature's assistants! So save those seeds, respect all living things, and enjoy the wonder of it all.

And remember: You're a part of nature, too!

Only a wise child can understand
the language of flowers and plants.

Helen Keller

YOU ARE PART OF NATURE, TOO.

This book is ended, but the gifts you get from gardening will
keep on coming.

Of course, you can't see or hold or eat the best gifts of all —
patience, knowledge, appreciation, and fun. Put them together
and you've got the highest prize there is — wisdom.

 # INDEX

More Good Books from
WILLIAMSON PUBLISHING

Williamson books are available from your bookseller or directly from Williamson Publishing. Please see last page for ordering information or to visit our website. Thank you.

THE ORIGINAL WILLIAMSON'S *KIDS CAN!*® BOOKS ...

The following *Kids Can!*® books for ages 7 to 14 are each 144 to 176 pages, fully illustrated, trade paper, 11 x 8 ½, $12.95 US.

☆ American Bookseller Pick of the Lists
☆ 2000 American Institute of Physics Science Writing Award
☆ Parents' Choice Honor Award

GIZMOS & GADGETS
Creating Science Contraptions that Work (& Knowing Why)
BY JILL FRANKEL HAUSER

☆ American Bookseller Pick of the Lists
☆ Oppenheim Toy Portfolio Best Book Award
☆ Teachers' Choice Award

SUPER SCIENCE CONCOCTIONS
50 Mysterious Mixtures for Fabulous Fun
BY JILL FRANKEL HAUSER

☆ American Bookseller Pick of the Lists
☆ Parents' Choice Recommended

ADVENTURES IN ART
Arts & Crafts Experiences for 8- to 13-Year-Olds
BY SUSAN MILORD

☆ Parents Choice Silver Honor Award

THE KIDS' NATURAL HISTORY BOOK
Making Dinos, Fossils, Mammoths & More!
BY JUDY PRESS

☆ American Bookseller Pick of the Lists
☆ Oppenheim Toy Portfolio Best Book Award

THE KIDS' SCIENCE BOOK
Creative Experiences for Hands-On Fun
BY ROBERT HIRSCHFELD & NANCY WHITE

☆ Parents' Choice Gold Award
☆ Benjamin Franklin Best Juvenile Nonfiction Award

KIDS MAKE MUSIC!
Clapping & Tapping from Bach to Rock
BY AVERY HART AND PAUL MANTELL

☆ American Bookseller Pick of the Lists
☆ Dr. Toy Best Vacation Product

KIDS' CRAZY ART CONCOCTIONS
50 Mysterious Mixtures for Art & Craft Fun
BY JILL FRANKEL HAUSER

☆ Parents' Choice Recommended

KIDS' ART WORKS!
Creating with Color, Design, Texture & More
BY SANDI HENRY

JAZZY JEWELRY
Power Beads, Crystals, Chokers, & Illusion and Tattoo Styles
BY DIANE BAKER

☆ Selection of Book-of-the-Month; Scholastic Book Clubs

KIDS COOK!
Fabulous Food for the Whole Family
BY SARAH WILLIAMSON & ZACHARY WILLIAMSON

☆ Parents' Choice Recommended

THE KIDS' BOOK OF WEATHER FORECASTING
BY MARK BREEN AND KATHLEEN FRIESTAD